Race, Culture, and the City

SUNY Series, Teacher Empowerment and School Reform
Henry A. Giroux and Peter L. McLaren, Editors

Race, Culture, and the City

A Pedagogy for
Black Urban Struggle

Stephen Nathan Haymes

State University of New York Press

Published by
State University of New York Press, Albany

© 1995 State University of New York

For information, address State University of New York
Press, State University Plaza, Albany, N.Y., 12246

Production by E. Moore
Marketing by Fran Keneston

Library of Congress Cataloging-in-Publication Data

Haymes, Stephen Nathan.
    Race, culture, and the city : a pedagogy for Black urban struggle
/ Stephen Nathan Haymes ; forward by Cynthia Hamilton ; introduction
by Henry A. Giroux and Peter McLaren.
        p.   cm. — (SUNY series, teacher empowerment and school
reform)
    Includes bibliographical references (p.   ) and index.
    ISBN 0-7914-2383-2 (alk. paper). — ISBN 0-7914-2384-0 (pbk. :
alk. paper)
    1. Afro-Americans—Education. 2. Education, Urban—United States.
3. Critical pedagogy—United States. 4. Educational anthropology-
-United States. I. Title. II. Series: Teacher empowerment and
school reform.
LB2717.H39 1995
370'.8996073—dc20   LC
                         2717   94-11213
                         .H39   CIP
                         1995

10 9 8 7 6 5 4 3 2

To my parents,
Nathanial and Bernice Haymes,
and my sister and brothers

Contents

Preface

This analysis comes at a critical moment in the history of black America. As we view the collapsed ruins of what once were viable communities (Harlem, Chicago's southside, Philadelphia, etc.) with their own very special history and meaning, not only for black Americans but throughout the diaspora, a sense of despair and hopelessness has descended and with it a plethora of social ills. Professor Haymes addresses not only the sense of loss which has resulted but also what must be done to reclaim the meaning of our lives. This theoretical analysis should be seen as a practical guide by cultural workers, educators, and advocacy planners. By building the bridge linking the social/cultural to the physical environment Professor Haymes is able to approach issues and ideas in a new and innovative way. By calling for a "pedagogy of resistance" he forces us to reclaim the work of Franz Fanon who called on the oppressed to discover their identity by throwing off the shackles of domination.

In a very practical sense this means reclaiming what has been lost both to bulldozers and to consumer culture. It means reclaiming, reshaping, rebuilding, a very difficult task in an ahistorical era, in which commercial images are more familiar than fact.

At a time when all public figures claim education, Professor Haymes calls for "critical pedagogy" as a tool to reclaim memory. Memory is a very important first step for the old and the young, but for black Americans it is the difficult first step to recovery. Here we must seek meaning in the past, though not uncritically. This process is not always easy. As we look at the conditions of daily life (overcrowding, life on the street, etc.) we must ask what these conditions make us as a people, as individuals.

What has altered our ability to find alternative meaning in the different conditions we experience? It means looking for meaning where and when it hurts. Haymes calls on us to give meaning to our urbanness, to reclaim spaces and make them home once more. Black Americans should no longer take our difference from or sameness with white America for granted. Through defining what exists we can move on to accept or reject, but more important we can learn to construct an identity from which new action, behavior, praxis, is possible.

This is an analysis which leaves us with hope, which instructs us to act, to be ourselves once again. But first we must discover what that means.

CYNTHIA M. HAMILTON
UNIVERSITY OF RHODE ISLAND

Series Editors' Introduction

In *Race, Culture, and the City: A Pedagogy for Black Urban Struggle*, Stephen Haymes is concerned, first and foremost, with the racializing of urban space from the standpoint of white supremacist ideologies that primitivize and pathologize black bodies, that discursively constitute black urban populations through jungle metaphors and racist myths surrounding the exotic black subject, and that lead to forms of black self-contempt. Of particular interest to Haymes is the means by which black subjectivities are produced within texts and subtexts of urban cultural myths, material development, and social practices within urban "postmodernized" spaces. With an impressive sweep of scholarship ranging from neo-Marxist analysis to post-structuralist accounts of self and social formation, Haymes is able to capture the pain suffered and the struggle and hope exercised by African-Americans in contemporary urban settings where African-American communities serve as zones of contest between dominant discursive practices that identify black people as dangerous Others and illuminate the survival strategies of black people against the still prevalent practices of white racism, hatred, and terror.

Haymes warns his readers that we inhabit an era in which deindustrialization is transforming African-American city dwellers into an expendable surplus population of little or not use to the larger economy—a population ruthlessly condemned by white patriarchal culture because it does not generate wealth. This is not surprising, Haymes argues, when you consider that the new matrix for urban stability for a society in ruins has become upscale consumer-oriented living, leisure, and entertainment for mostly new white middle class. From the vantage point of critical social theory, Haymes is able to examine how, in contemporary urban settings, the free-market values of white entrepreneurialism have disrupted and unsettled the bonds of trust, friendship, and solidarity that had once been common to black communities and black cultures. He pays specific attention to the warehousing of economically disenfranchised African-Americans and the racialization of residential and institutional spaces where African-Americans are differentially defined by the discourses and social practices of post-industrial capitalism—practices in which profit making is by and large protected from public accountability. Haymes does not retreat from the uncomfortable reality that in some cases blacks themselves have become complicitous in converting the public spaces of the ghetto into private spaces of consumption.

Haymes follows Paul Gilroy in identifying black culture as a "social movement" that exists outside the immediate process of production and that must be understood to be organized around the production of meaning, desire, affect, corporeality, and identity. Accordingly, Haymes argues that greater attention must be paid to the production of desire with post-industrial capitalism than to the instrumental objectives of corporatist class politics.

Haymes's bold and sensitive analysis attempts to explain the impact of consumer-oriented capitalism on black identity politics. He is at pains to describe the devastating effects of the binary logic of the white racist imagination on the production of black culture and the biologization of black identity in postmodern "spacialized" urban arenas where Euro-Americans are disproportionately privileged. Haymes addresses with keen insight and impressive scholarship the impact of white consumer culture on the construction of black subjectivity, especially in terms of the way in which the consumer culture of the white middle class constructs an urban spatial arrangement that transforms the "black ghetto" into pleasure spaces for white middle-class consumption. These spaces of pleasure are tied inexorably to the ideology of the free market. There are gentrified neighborhoods in which whites consume black music, dance, sports, and fashion with the aid of their private security systems, forms of electronic surveillance, and the police.

One of many remarkable aspects of *Race, Culture, and the City* is the way in which Haymes develops an antiessentialist identity politics and black cultural politics for urban public spaces related to what he calls "place-making" practices. The place-making practices of urban blacks differ from those of the white middle class. White institutionalized practices are able to both symbolically and materially destroy the "homeplaces" of inner-city blacks through the ideological and social practices of white developers, landowners, media, politicians, banks, and corporations.

Through a discussion of architecture, urban planning, and social movements, Haymes brilliantly explores the way place-making practices of blacks are politically and culturally constituted as a threat to tradition. For Haymes, spaces and places are zones of contest between Euro-Americans and people of color. Certain "unruly" populations such as African-Americans and Latinos are discursively constructed through the racialization of their spaces of habitat. Struggles over the representation and control of spaces have drastic consequences for black populations when seen in the light of the politics of urban renewal, the criminalization of black inner-city youth, the gentrification of black and Latino neighborhoods, the establishment of narcotic enforcement zones in places such as south central Los Angeles, and the ideology of architectural redevelopment.

Related to Haymes's concept of place-making is his development of a "pedagogy of place" that draws on the tradition of critical pedagogy to develop counterpublic spheres of resistance and social transformation. Haymes is particularly interested in and proves exceptionally capable of rethinking the concept of counterpublic spheres which will enable African-Americans to reclaim the ideological and material conditions for organizing their own experiences and forging political and cultural practices to allow them both to interpret and to change social reality in ways that lead to liberation. Haymes's pedagogical project is designed to be made operative in specific urban contexts of city life to provide the conditions for African-Americans to unsettle and overturn dominant representations of blackness and uses of urban space. Haymes argues that the loss of place-making memories by black populations in the inner city needs to be understood in terms of how dominant uses of urban space and the politics of representing black urban populations have been naturalized by white cultural meanings. Haymes's pedagogy of place enables those conditions to be created whereby African-Americans can reclaim and recontextualize their popular memories and histories of place making around the struggle over urban territory, space, and identity. Such a pedagogy is located in the ways that urban black populations view the process of redevelopment and the creation of racialized spaces and racialized Others.

Calling for a pedagogy of place that moves beyond the tension between assimilationist and Afrocentric perspectives, Haymes expands his idea of pedagogy to include a project of decolonization designed to resist the colonizing project of white supremacist culture and the Western humanist tradition, both of which serve to contain difference by creating an essentialist and unified notion of black racial identity predicated upon demonic myths of black Otherness. Because of its singular ability to reconfigure the very parameters of the debate surrounding Otherness, and its success at reframing in new and urgent pedagogical terms the struggle for our urban centers, *Race, Culture, and the City* is a book that demands a careful reading by educators, urban policy makers, social workers, and school administrators.

Stephen Haymes is part of a new generation of gifted transdisciplinary scholars who are able to bring new categories and frameworks of analysis to the politics of urban

struggle. In advancing our current understandings of pedagogy, place, and difference, Haymes both relocates and rear-
ticulates the project of critical pedagogy so that it is able
to address new sets of problems and offer new possibilities
for urban struggle. What is at stake in Haymes's work is
nothing less than the reconstitution of the struggle for a
black politics of liberation. It is a politics that Euro-
Americans, Latinos, Asians, Native Americans, and others
should take seriously, because within such a politics
Haymes prepares for us a "place" from which we can all
create a common ground of struggle.

PETER MCLAREN AND HENRY A. GIROUX

Acknowledgments

This book would not have been completed without the support of many people. First I would like to thank my wife and friend, Maria Vidal de Haymes, for her advice and patience, and my two children, Maceo Dubois and Gabriela Soujouner, who was born during the period I was writing this book. Both sustained me with their love and much-needed interruptions. I want to thank the series editors, Henry Giroux and Peter McLaren for their support and interest in my work. Also, I want to thank my undergraduate mentor Cynthia Hamilton who has helped me greatly in thinking through various ideas contained in this book, and whose work has inspired my own. I also wish to acknowledge Valeri Collier, Judith Wittner, Joe Kincheloe, Rory Ong, Talmadge Wright, Carol Harding, and Suzette Speight for their moral support and encouragement. I am also grateful to Susanne Galiger and Nancy McCabe, graduate students in the School of Education at Loyola University-Chicago, for their insightful discussion and enthusiasm.

I also want to thank my editor at State University of New York Press, Priscilla Ross, who has been supportive as well as thorough and thoughtful.

Chapter One

Race, Culture, and the City: An Introduction

Introduction: Pedagogy and Urban Space

Race, Culture, and the City: A Pedagogy of Place for Black Urban Struggle argues for the necessity of developing a pedagogy of black urban resistance, which I define in relation to a "pedagogy of place." Though the relationship of "place" to pedagogy has largely been ignored in the study of education, the limited work that has been done has been greatly influenced by the spatial concepts of contemporary critical social theory including critical postmodernism, postcolonialism, feminist cultural studies, and black cultural studies. In *Postmodern Geographies* Edward W. Soja points out that geography plays a role in the making of history. He states: "A distinctively postmodern and critical human geography is taking shape, brashly reasserting the interpretive significance of space in the historically privileged confines of contemporary critical thought" (1990:11). Michael

Keith and Steve Pile in *Place and the Politics of Identity* similarly argue that critical social theory has drawn on "spatial metaphors," such as position, location, situation, mapping; geometrics of domination, centre-margin, open-closed, inside-outside, global-local; liminal space, third space, not-space, impossible space; the city" (1994:1). Both Soja and Keith and Pile assert that space has both a material and an interpretive quality, which Soja describes as "actually lived and socially created spatiality, concrete and abstract at the same time, the habitus of social practices" (1990:18).

This spatialization of contemporary critical social theory has influenced the way critical pedagogists think about pedagogy. However, I would qualify this by saying that Paulo Freire's earlier work *Pedagogy of the Oppressed* predates this influence. Freire is aware that all pedagogies are situated in place, in the spatially configured lived and interpretive experiences of the learner. In talking about a pedagogy that addresses the particular situation of the oppressed Freire writes:

> Men [and women], as beings "in a situation," find themselves rooted in temporal-spatial conditions which mark them and which they also mark. They will tend to reflect on their own "situationality" to the extent that they are challenged by it to act upon it. Men and [women] are because they are in a situation. And they will be more the more they not only critically reflect upon their existence but critically act upon it. (1970:100)

This aspect of Freire has been taken up and expanded on by Henry Giroux (1992a; 1993; 1994), Peter McLaren (1993a; 1993b; 1993c; 1993d;1994), and other critical pedagogists who argue that for the marginalized and oppressed to critically reflect and act upon their existence pedagogy must be informed by a "politics of location." When pedagogy is defined in relation to "locationality" "at question is the issue of who speaks, under what conditions, for whom, and how knowledge is constructed and translated within and between different communities located within asymmetrical relations of power" (Giroux, 1992a:2).

Although Freire and other critical pedagogists do not specifically focus on the city, their insights into how a "politics of location" or a "politics of place" can inform pedagogy is important for understanding the link between pedagogy and the production of urban meaning. *Race, Culture, and the City* asserts that pedagogy must be linked to how individuals and collectivities make and take up culture in the production of public spaces in the city, with particular emphasis on how they use and assign meaning to public spaces within unequal relations of power in an effort to "make place." A critical pedagogy of urban place and struggle therefore must take up how the manufacturing of urban meanings structures our perceptions about different living spaces and the political and ethical consequences of those meanings on both the spaces and the people that live in them.

The Social Construction of the City

The basic premise of *Race, Culture, and City* is that cultural images and historical images have as much influence on the spatial form of the city as do economics (Castells, 1983; Saunders, 1986; Langer, 1984). Manuel Castells states: "Because society is structured around conflicting positions which define alternative values and interests, so the production of space and cities will be, too" (1983:xvi). Similarly, Folch-Serra points out that "human agents wield agency through language [and that] this agency creates landscapes through metaphors . . . whose outcome is the building of roads, towns, and cultures. Landscapes can be regarded as places where social, historical, and geographical conditions allow different voices to express themselves" (1990:255). Cityscapes are therefore constitutive of many different voices and living spaces that have relations between them. Foucault calls these heterogeneous and relational spaces "heterotopias," denoting that they are capable of being "juxtaposed to one another, set off against one another as a sort of configuration" (Soja, 1990:19-20). His concept of a heterotopia is useful for understanding how some spaces get portrayed as "normal" and "ordered" at the expense of constructing others as "abnormal" and "disordered" (Soja, 1990:17).

In the context of American cities the category of "race" is used metaphorically as a way to juxtapose the different "social spaces" that make up the urban landscape, describing some as "normal" and "ordered" and others as not. Malcolm Cross and Michael Keith remark that "[r]ace is a privileged metaphor through which the confused text of the city is rendered comprehensible" (1993:9). They argue that "our way of seeing cities and thinking about cities this sense of urbanism is deeply racialized (1993:9). It is in this "racialized urbanism" that blackness is the urban Other, the disordered and the dangerous. This portrayal of blackness in urban mythology is central to the social construction of the city as a representation of the id and the superego, a "juxtaposition of primitive urge and civilizing consciousness" (Wilson cited in Cross and Keith, 1993:9). In this urban mythology black and white represent the id and superego respectively. It has been this urban mythology that has identified blacks with disorder and danger in the city. Gerald Suttles accepts this mythology while arguing that it provides the city with "cognitive maps" to "regulate spatial movement and locational possibilities" (1972:23). Suttles believes that "cognitive maps" are necessary for white "ethnic" neighborhoods to defend themselves from their enemies—the urban Other. Their enemies, in Suttles' words, are "people who fall short of existing standards that attest to their trustworthiness and self-restraint. Typically, these are poor people from a low-status minority group " (1968:5). It is from this vantage point that Suttles defines what he means by *cognitive maps*:

> Cognitive maps provide a set of social categories for
> differentiating between those people with whom one

can or cannot safely associate and for defining the concrete groupings within which certain levels of social contact and cohesion obtain. These cognitive maps, then, are a creative imposition on the city and useful because they provide a final solution to decision making where there are often no other clear cutoff points for determining how far social contacts should go. (1972:22)

The white supremacist thinking and attitudes that undergird urban mythologies about blacks have resulted in their spatial regulation and control in cities. Put another way, contemporary urban forms are the spatial expression of racialized values or what some have referred to as the "urban realization of the ideology of apartheid" (Cross and Keith, 1993:11). Douglas Massey and Nancy Denton in *American Apartheid* argue that the continued high levels of residential segregation experienced by blacks in American cities is an example of this ideology actualized in urban form. Racial prejudice and discriminatory real estate practices designed to insulate whites from blacks have been the cause of black residential segregation (Massey and Denton, 1993). Their study shows that post-world-war racial prejudice and discrimination in the housing market by whites established today's persistent patterns of black residential segregation. The principle of racial exclusion was practiced through restrictive covenants and deeds employed by neighborhood "improvement" associations and social pressure applied to realtors, property owners, and public officials (Massey and Denton, 1993:58).

Massey and Denton add that until 1950 federally sponsored mortgage programs also reinforced racial exclusion in that FHA and VA mortgages went to white middle-class suburbs, while very few were awarded to black neighborhoods in the inner city. The rationale given for this practice was that increased black population would drive down property values therefore increasing the risk involved in backing the loans. Furthermore, Massey and Denton argued that the FHA "recommended the use and application of racially restrictive covenants as a means of ensuring the security of neighborhoods and did not change this recommendation until 1950" (1993:54). Subsequently, the racially discriminatory practices of federally sponsored mortgage programs resulted in high levels of black residential segregation, as well as encouraged private lending institutions to not make loans to black inner-city neighborhoods. The consequence of disinvestment in black central-city neighborhoods at the expense of middle-class white suburbs were "steep declines in property values and a pattern of disrepair, deterioration, vacancy, and abandonment" (Massey and Denton, 1993:55).

Fearful that this decline would spill over into adjacent white communities, harming white business districts and elite institutions, local white urban elites during the 1950s and 1960s through downtown redevelopment "manipulated housing and urban renewal legislation to carry out widespread slum clearance (Massey and Denton, 1993:55-56). Slum clearance as defined and practiced by the local white urban elites meant the tearing down of black neighborhoods adjacent to white areas and converting them to other uses, the intended goal being to block the expansion of the "ghetto." According to Massey and Denton, those displaced because of urban renewal were either permanently dislocated into other crowded "ghetto neighborhoods" or relocated to high-density tower public housing projects, built for the specific purpose of warehousing poor blacks:

> By 1970, after two decades of urban renewal, public housing projects in most large cities had become black reservations, highly segregated from the rest of society and characterized by extreme social isolation. The replacement of low-density slums with high-density towers of poor families also reduced the class diversity of the ghetto and brought about a geographic concentration of poverty that was previously unimaginable. This new segregation of blacks—in

economic as well as social terms—was the direct result of an unprecedented collaboration between local and national government. (1993:57)

What Massey and Denton's comment suggests is that black urban poverty is the outcome of black residential segregation and is therefore responsible for the emergence of the "urban underclass." However, they mistakenly point to how the residential segregation of blacks has resulted in their marginalization and isolation from white mainstream culture and values and that this has contributed to the lack of "black socioeconomic advancement and income growth" (1993:163). They point to how "the depth of isolation in the ghetto is evident in black speech patterns" and say that because of this "ghetto residents have come to speak a language that is increasingly remote from that spoken by American whites" (1993:162).

The persistence of "black speech patterns" because of the sociocultural isolation imposed on blacks by residential segregation is believed by Massey and Denton to be the reason for low educational achievement and the lack of employment opportunities. Also mentioned is that "black speech patterns" reflect the supposed values that underlie forms of black cultural identity that arise from residential segregation and that these values are "defined in opposition to the basic ideals and values of American society" (1993:167). It is argued that "black identity" and "black street culture" are at variance with mainstream white cultural values such as self-reliance, hard work, sobriety, and sacrifice and that this has led to the "legitimat[ing] of certain behaviors prevalent with the black community that would otherwise be held in contempt by white society" (1993:167). Referring to "black street culture," Massey and Denton argue that black residential segregation has resulted in an "autonomous cultural system" (1993:172). They claim that it is a cultural system that devalues work, marriage, and family formation but promotes male joblessness, teenage motherhood, single parenthood, alcoholism, drug abuse, crime, violence, and school failure (1993:162-78). According Massey and Denton, it is "black street culture" perpetuated by black residential segregation that has produced America's huge black "urban underclass." Their solution is a dismantling of the "ghetto" (1993:236).

What is interesting, Massey and Denton do not consider geographical areas concentrated with whites as "racially" hypersegregated. Seldom do they identify the so-called broader society or white society or American society in terms of a "racially" defined geographical space, and when they do it is rarely mentioned as "white residential segregation." In addition, they unquestioningly attribute differences between black and white "ghettos" (I use the term *ghetto* to denote white middle-class neighborhoods as well since they are segregated), between the value placed on self-reliance, hard work, sobriety, and sacrifice, and the belief that these principles will bring monetary reward and economic advancement, to race and culture rather than to mainstream white privilege and domination. Massey and Denton, through their ideological construction of residential segregation, racialize the residential spaces of blacks but not whites. What they have done is to transpose racial identity, or stereotypical black images of disruptive behavior, attitudes, and values, on to residential location. Susan Smith defines this maneuver by whites as the "racialization of residential space" through the imagery of racial segregation:

> When referring to the racialization of residential space, I mean the process by which residential location is taken as an index of the attitudes, values, behavioral inclinations and social norms of the kinds of people who are assumed to live in particular "black" or "white," inner city or suburban, neighborhoods. Once the "black inner city" is isolated in this way, the image of racial segregation is mustered as spurious evidence of the supposedly natural origins of social ("racial") differentiation. (1993:133)

It is the imagery of racial segregation, the transposing of white supremacist representations of black identity on to residential space, that has reinforced the notion that the problems experienced by black people are sharply bounded in space (Smith, 1993:134). Smith states, "The social construction of racial segregation portrays urban deprivation as a moral problem, deflecting attention away from the power structures creating and sustaining the inequalities dividing black and white [Americans]" (1993:136). The bounding of the problems experienced by blacks in space, Smith observes, means that the political and economic contradictions of black subjugation and white domination and privilege get defined as technical and administrative problems, as policy recommendations that support racial desegregation and the dismantling of black urban settlements.

The Social Construction of Black Urban Struggle

> The inner city communities combat the segregated space of ethnic fragmentation, cultural strangeness, and economic overexploitation of the new post-industrial city with the defense of their identity, the preservation of their culture, the search for their roots, and the marking out of their newly acquired territory. Sometimes, also, they display their rage, and attempt to devastate the institutions that they believe devastate their daily lives. (Castells, 1983:317)

With Castells' comment in mind, one way to begin to understand the social construction of black urban struggles is by looking at how black urban communities resist white supremacists' urban meanings and urban forms by constructing alternative images and representations of place. By doing so, urban blacks construct self-definitions; their making of place is tied to the construction of their social identity as blacks. Related to this is the assumption that for poor and working-class black urban communities the making of place has been significant in forging a politics of struggle or resistance. Referring to the black urban revolts of the 1960s, Manuel Castells in *The City and the Grassroots* notes that "the ghetto territory became a significant space for the black community as the material basis of social organization, cultural identity and political power" (1983:49-54). Castells argues that the relationship between black geographical concentration and the urban revolts was "analogous with the concentration of industrial workers in large factories being indispensable to the formation of the labor movement" (1983:54). In agreement with Castells, Cynthia Hamilton argues that the massive black migration from the rural South to southern and northern cities, consequently resulting in the geographical concentration of blacks, not only was the basis for strong black urban communities that evolved and flourished through the world wars, it may have been the spark for the civil rights movement:

> Many say this new demographic arrangement may have been a spark for the civil rights movement. It is clear that the spatial configuration of that period was an asset to political organizing and protest. Greater concentration of the population strengthened community bonds and institutions and even provided the basis for electoral strength after the Voting Rights Act of 1965. (1991:29)

It is within this context that place making is tied to the idea that places are significant because we assign meaning to them in relation to our specific projects. I will argue that this concept is linked with self-definition or identity formation. However, I might add that projects are shaped by experiences in everyday life, so that within black urban communities place making and therefore the production of public spaces is linked with day-to-day survival. But it is within the realm of day-to-day life, of daily survival, that black urban communities create "public spaces" that allow them to develop self-definitions or social identities that are linked to a consciousness and politics of resistance. A. Sivanandan in *Communities of Resistance: Writings on Black Struggles for Socialism* suggests this relationship among daily survival, consciousness, and black urban resistance when he writes,

> By their very location, the underclass are the most difficult to organize in the old sense of organization. They do not submit to the type of trade union regimen which operates for the straight "official" workforce. . . . They come together over everyday cases of hardship to help each other's families, setting up informal community centres. . . . Relegated to a concrete ghetto and deprived of basic amenities and services, jobless for the most part and left open to crime, the inhabitants came together to create a life for themselves. They set up a nursery, provided meals and a meeting place for pensioners, established a recreation centre for youth and build up in the process, a political culture [of resistance]. These are not great big things they do, but they are the sort of organic communities of resistance that, in a sense, were prefigured in the black struggles of the 1960s and 1970s and the insurrections of 1981 and 1985. (1990:52)

Although Sivanandan's comments mainly address contemporary black urban struggles in Britain, he provides insight into black urban struggles in the United States, particularly as they relate to the particular form of political organizing by poor and working-class black urban communities. Of significance is the way in which the political organizing of these communities is linked to developing day-to-day strategies and networks of survival and self-reliance. Though Carol Stack in *All of Our Kin: Strategies for Survival in a Black Community* does not focus like Sivanandan on how strategies and networks of self-reliance become the basis for political organizing, she does draw

attention to how these strategies and networks are the basis
for daily survival for black urban communities in the United
States. In addition, she argues that unlike the mainstream
white free-market values of individualism, competitiveness,
and materialism, the value system that undergirds the survival networks of poor and working-class black urban communities is based on what she calls an "ethic of cooperation." Stack observes, "They share with one another
because of the urgency of their needs. Alliances between
individuals are created around the clock as kin and friends
exchange and give and obligate one another" (1974:32). The
point is that through networks and strategies of survival
black urban communities develop bonds of trust, friendship, and solidarity.

However, Stack's discussion assumes that "black solidarity" is based on some utilitarian logic, which presumes
that relationships between blacks are entered into on the
basis of economic self-interest. If this is the case, if survival
strategies and networks are simply guided by a utilitarian
logic, why do blacks choose to participate in these networks
with blacks and not with whites. The question then is to
what extend does black culture play a role in the formation
of black solidarity? As St. Clair Drake and Horace Cayton
remind us in their classic *Black Metropolis*, unlike the
"gilded sections of the black neighborhood in Chicago,
lower-class sections "had a warm and familiar ghetto subculture that flourished through ribs, shrimp, chicken, juke
box, soul and swager." What Drake and Cayton's observa-
tions tell us is that the bonds of trust, friendship, and solidarity that are constitutive of black survival networks are
shaped by black culture. This means that to understand
black solidarity we must analyze the category of black culture.

One way to analyze black culture is to interpret it as a
social movement; this makes more explicit the intersec-
tion between culture, political action, and organization. The
term *social movement* is distinguished from those social
and political collectivities that are based on the political

economy of the workplace, such as the labor movement. Put another way, social movements "are located outside the immediate process of production, and consequently require the reappropriation of space, time and of relationships between individuals in their day to day lives" (Gilroy, 1991:224). It is outside the workplace, the capital-labor contradiction, that social movements transform economic and extra-economic modes of subordination (Gilroy, 1992). For example, in post-industrial capitalist society urban blacks constitute a surplus population, an expendable population that is no longer useful to capitalist economic production. Mass urban black unemployment and underemployment, due to white racism and the automation and cybernation of the workplace, suggests that the "factory" is not the major site from which urban blacks develop black consciousness and solidarity. The black power movement of the 1970s recognized this by suggesting that the geographical space of the city was essential for the emergence of "black power consciousness" (Allen, 1967; Boggs, 1970; Carmichael and Hamilton, 1967; Bush, 1984; Marable, 1991).

It is in the "spaces of the ghetto" then that black consciousness and solidarity are mostly formed. Alberto Melucci argues that one of the characteristics of contemporary social movements is their alternative public spaces, which he describes as "submerged networks." According to Melucci, these networks are where actors of social movements invest "in the experimentation and practice of new cultural models, forms of relationships and alternative perceptions of the world" (1989:60). In this way, the organizational form of a social movement is itself the message, a symbolic challenge to the dominant codes" (Melucci, 1989:60). This means, then, that the organizational forms of social movements are in Melucci's words "self-referential"; they "are not just instrumental for their goals; they are a goal in themselves" (1989:60). In a sense, black settlement space is the location from which urban blacks construct alternative experiences of time, space, and interpersonal relationships or community, an alternative culture to that of white supremacist capitalist patriarchy.

I do not wish to imply that black settlement spaces or "black ghettos" are self-contained and therefore isolated from the processes of post-industrial capitalism. Instead, my argument is that the particular "mode of production" of post-industrial capitalism has had much influence on the production of black culture within the spaces of the inner city. This is because one of the distinguishing features of post-industrial capitalist society is the dominance of elec-tronic-information technologies; in other words, "informa-tion has become the core resource" (Melucci, 1989:185). Acknowledging this, Melucci presents the implication of this for human consciousness and subjectivity in what he calls "complex societies":

> Our access to reality is facilitated and shaped by the conscious production and control of information. "Forms" or images produced through perception and cognition increasingly organize our relationship to the material and communicative environment in which we live. The transformation of natural resources into commodities has come to depend on the production and control of these cognitive and communicative "forms." Power based upon mate-rial production is therefore no longer central. (1989:185)

In Chapter 2 of *Race, Culture, and the City*, I will elabo-rate on the consequences of this for contemporary black con-sciousness and subjectivity. In post-industrial capitalism the "mode of production," cultural/symbolic production, has become more dominant within the economic/material pro-ductive sphere. Alain Tourine points out that this has resulted "in the production of symbolic goods that modify values, needs, representations, more so than "the produc-tion of material goods or even of services" (1988:104). Industrial society, Tourine observes, "had transformed the means of production; post-industrial society changes the ends of production, that is culture" (1988:104). These changes have meant that the terrain for constructing political action is now qualitatively different than the era of industrial capitalism. That is to say, political action has moved from the instrumental objectives of corporatist class politics, the winning of political power, toward "control of a field of autonomy or independence vis a vis the system and the immediate satisfaction of collective desires" (Gilroy, 1991:226). The models of management, production, organization, distribution, and consumption of state bureaucracies and capitalist corporations, models that control and regulate "areas of self-definition, emotional relationships, sexuality and biological needs" (Melucci, 1989:46), are challenged by the identity politics of social movements. Therefore, in post-industrial capitalist society the focus of social movements is on social identity. Melucci further elaborates this point by suggesting that the identity politics of social movements are focused on mobilizing and controlling their own action:

> There are aspects of the action through which actors signal and expose problems that concern the means of production and distribution of resources of meaning. The actors mobilize to regain control of their own action. They try to reclaim the right to define themselves against the criteria of identification determined by an anonymous power and system of regulation that penetrates the area of "internal nature." (1989:189)

This category of social movement, although inseparable, is analytically distinguishable from collective mobilization. More specifically, mobilizations such as strikes, civil disobedience, marches, and rebellions are visible events or outcomes of action, and to focus simply at the level of mobilization is to ignore how action is itself produced. As briefly mentioned above, social movements are principally organized around the production of meaning, desire, affect, corporeality, and identity. Related to this point is that "the black social movement was the first to expand the concerns of politics to the social, to the terrain of everyday life" (Omi and Winant, 1987). Others have made a similar point by arguing that "the politics of identity can learn much from a closer engagement with the experiences of racialized minorities" (Cross and Keith 1993:22). Malcolm Cross and Michael Keith have noted: "The recently discovered post-modern condition of marginality and fragmentation, positively signified, has been lived and worked through for the last 40 years, and more by racialized minorities in post-metropolitian economies" (1993:22). And in terms of cultural theory, they argue that Frantz Fanon's psychoanalytic work was a key reference point for British and American blacks in addressing "the inextricable interplay of social context of oppression and resistance in the internalization of complex identities in the formation of self (Cross and Keith, 1993:23).

Another concern of Chapter 2 is the impact of a consumer-oriented capitalism on black identity politics. This is of particular concern in that consumer capitalism is informed by mainstream white culture's exotic interest in black culture. The commodification of black culture, in a society dominated by the white racist imagination, has transformed it from an outwardly oriented culture of joy— that fosters kindness, love, caring, service, solidarity, and the struggle for justice—to an inwardly oriented culture of pleasure that promotes the market values of individualism, materialism, and competiveness (Dent, 1992:1). One of the questions addressed in Chapter 2 is related to the effects of consumer-oriented capitalism on black self-definition since it is informed by white supremacist culture. Second, how have the effects of internalized racism, the result of the dominance of white supremacist ideology, combined with a consumer-oriented capitalist value system of competitiveness, materialism, and individualism affected black solidarity in the city?

Johnathan Kozol in *Savage Inequalities* argues that there is a correspondence between the rise of black inner-city crime and the intentional aggressive promotion through advertisement of "black" consumerism by U.S. corporations. Kozol states: "The manufacturing of desire for commodities that children of low income can't afford pushes them to underground economies and crime to find the money to appease the longings we have often fostered" (1991:191). Others show how the white supremacist ideology that signifies consumer culture, that makes blackness and black culture a metaphor for pleasure and desire, is damaging to the black psyche and encourages destructive forms of behavior, such as black-on-black violence and covert suicide through drugs (hooks and West, 1991; hooks, 1993; Marable, 1992a; West, 1991b, Kozol, 1992; Nightingale, 1994). These questions and issues are of import given Melucci's insights regarding the relationship of culture to the production of action in post-industrial capitalist society. He states that

> in the current period, society's capacity to intervene in the production of meaning extends to those areas which previously escaped control and regulation: areas of self-definition, emotional relationships, sexuality and biological needs. (1989:33)

In addition to addressing the destructiveness of mainstream white consumer culture on black culture and black identity, Chapter 2 will also examine the contradictory way in which black cultural workers have resisted white racist images and representations of the "black body" by taking up what Peter McLaren calls a "politics of the flesh." As Paul Gilroy states: "Blacks who live in the castle of their skin and have struggled to escape the biologization of their socially and politically constructed subordination are already sensitive to this issue. The attempt to articulate blackness as an historical rather than as a natural category confronts it directly" (1991:226). Black cultural workers have confronted this biologization directly or have reappropriated it to fashion a culture of resistance. The potential of black cultural politics to reinforce white supremacy and black self-contempt—in the form of black male misogyny or black middle-class hatred of lower-class—will also be discussed.

Chapter 3 of *Race, Culture, and the City* examines how the consumer culture of the white middle-class produces a spatial arrangement in cities that transforms the public spaces of "black ghetto" described by bell hooks as "homplaces" into private spaces or "pleasure spaces" for white middle-class consumption. As Neil Smith has suggested, "We are witnessing the construction of an urban rather than a suburban dream" (1987:152). In post-industrial capitalist society, the dominance of electronic information technologies has made the cultural and symbolic a core resource in the production of consumer goods. However, this has been accompanied by disindustrialization, the making of an expendable surplus population, a new spatial reconfiguration of the city. Comparing South Central, Los Angeles to the "bantustans" in South Africa, Cynthia Hamilton in "Apartheid in an American City" clearly describes how the "urban dream" of the post-industrial capitalist city is removing the material or territorial basis of the black and Latino public sphere:

> Much like the bulldozing of black encampments on the fringe of Johannesburg or Durban, it can be argued, South Central, Los Angeles is inevitably slated by the historical process to be replaced without a trace: cleared land ready for development for a more prosperous—and probably whiter—class of people. For the large, unspoken malady affecting South Central stems from the idea that the land is valuable and the present tenants are not. This "bantustan," like its counterparts in South Africa, serves now only as a holding space for blacks and browns no longer of use to the larger economy.

Kristin Kiptiuch refers to the process Hamilton describes in South Central Los Angeles as "third worldizing at home." This concept metaphor she argues "names the effect of a process of exploitative incorporation and hegemonic domination—and its fierce contestation by subjugated peoples" (1991:88). The "third world," Koptiuch believes, "can no longer be geographically mapped off as a space separate from a seigneurial "first world." Describing the nation's major urban centers, she writes, "The shift towards desperation is apparent in the growing disparities between the dominant white population and the 'minority' population of the inner cities, and in growing similarities between the latter and people in countries conventionally associated with the 'third world'" (1991:89).

If within black inner-city communities networks of survival and self-relience produce public spaces, the converting of those spaces into private spaces of middle class consumption interrupts their continuation. Alexander Kluge (1991) refers to public spaces that are appropriated for private use as "pseudo-public spaces," those spaces that are privately owned and determined by the profit motive, making them bourgeois public spaces. He argues that the bourgeois public space represses debate, because it draws a false demarcation between the private and the public. This means that profit making is protected from public accountability because it is believed to be within the private domain, even though it depends on conditions that are publicly provided. The conclusion is that the bourgeois public space developed as a way for private interest to control "public activity." One major implication being that the private use of black public spaces represents an attempt to control the political dialogue about how the ghetto territory should be used and defined.

In Chapter 3, I will explore how this political dialogue about the use of public space in terms of privatization is framed in ways that glorify capitalist free market-ideology, and its belief that wealth is the result of individual hard work, and poverty is the result of laziness. Within a racialized society such as the United States, the subtext of this glorification is based on white supremacist assumptions about black people. This means that with regard to the logic of white supremacy black people are not materially better off than whites because their "black" bodies are assumed to lack self-regulation, self-discipline. Black culture is believed to be responsible for this behavior. Frantz Fanon called this form of racism "cultural racism" and said that it is a strategic maneuver by whites to fix black culture to nature, to the bodies of blacks.

The implication of naturalizing or essentializing black culture is that black public spaces are seen as pathological and in need of control (Goldberg, 1993). In the context of capitalist free-market ideology black "pathologies" are seen as the reason for black public spaces not being wealth generating, but wasteful and dependent upon public welfare. Within a white supremacist culture, such as in the United States, the concepts 'private' and 'public' now act as racialized metaphors; the private is equated with being "good" and "white," and the public with being "bad" and "black." Therefore, the rationale used to convert black public spaces into private spaces of middle-class consumption is based in part on this view. Nonetheless, the relation of free-market ideology to the cultural politics of race and racism, particularly as it relates to the privatizing of black public spaces, must also be understood in terms of the production of urban meanings. Chapter 3 therefore will examine the relationship between the cultural politics of race and racism and the production of urban meanings (Gilroy, 1991; Jefferies, 1993; Carby; 1993; Goldberg, 1993).

Predating the formation of large-scale black settlements in the city, the urban area was described as a jungle, where bestial, predatory values dominated. With the emergence of large black urban ghettos, the notion of the "city as a jungle" began to operate as a racist metaphor to describe inner-city blacks (Gilroy, 1991:228). Paul Gilroy notes: "It has contributed significantly to contemporary definitions of 'race,' particularly those which highlight the supposed primitivism and violence of black residents in inner-city areas" (1991:229). Related also is how the racializing of urban space around white supremacist notions of blackness has provided white urban political and economic elites and urban policy makers with an ideological alibi to dismantle black settlements and replace them with mainly white "gentrified" neighborhoods. Also implicit in the cultural forms of gentrified neighborhoods is a particular notion of place that appeals to white racial superiority. It is the symbolic construction of "white places" as civilized, rational, and orderly and "black places" as uncivilized, irrational, and disorderly that allows for police occupation and the removal of black people from their public spaces. This chapter will therefore critique the idea by Marxists that the political economy of capitalism is in the end the sole determiner of how urban space gets organized and that black urban social movements are either class movements in black skin, irrelevant to class politics in the city, or insignificant because the profit motive rather than race is believed to be the force behind spatial redevelopment (Harvey, 1989, 1990a, 1990b, 1991; Smith, 1984, 1986, 1987; Tabb and Sawer, 1978; Sorkin, 1991).

In Chapter 4, I will look at the relationship between black solidarity and pedagogy, particularly as it relates to black urban resistance and place making. The basic argument is that black solidarity is a product of black culture. And because culture is about the production of meanings, it shapes or frames the narratives and stories we use to define ourselves in relation to ourselves, others, and the world. Black culture in a sense must be understood from the perspective of how it pedagogically organizes black consciousness and black subjectivity. While the second chapter addresses mainstream white culture's exoticization of race with respect to consumption and its effects on black culture and black identity, Chapter 4 will take a closer look at the pedagogical production of urban meanings and how its racialized and racist subtext affects black culture and black consciousness.

Furthermore, Chapter 4 will examine the importance of critical pedagogy, in particular a pedagogy of black urban struggle, in terms of the racializing of urban space by main-stream white culture and its effects on black culture and black consciousness. Such a pedagogy is crucial given Mike Davis's argument that in American cities like Los Angeles the paramount axis of cultural conflict has always been about the construction/interpretation of the city myth, which enters the material landscape as a design for specula-tion and domination" (1990:23). This means that a pedagogy of black urban struggle must be linked to a "politics of loca-tion" and a "politics of voice" that understand the connec-tion between the formation of particular identities and the racial construction of urban myths, and what that means for the material landscape and development of the city.

In relation to race and the production of urban mytholo-gies, blacks have represented the id, the primitive urge. It is this representation that allowed mainstream whites to con-trol and regulate black popular culture for their pleasure and entertainment in the city. In fact, Cross and Keith argue that "the city of the post-industrial present" has produced a "new urbanism" which in the past two or three decades has restored the "cultural primacy of the urban in an era in which culture and the cash nexus seek out the city as play-ground" (1993:6). However, they add that the post-indus-trial capitalist city is a Eurocentric appropriation of post-modern culture. Cross and Keith state, "The archetypal postmodern city cannot be talked about in the Eurocentric specificity of the particular without allusion to urban oth-ers" (1993:8). It has been the postmodern city that has "digested, presented and represented [urban others] as racial-ized minorities" (Cross and Keith, 1993:8).

Mainstream white consumer culture is implicated in producing the racial subtext of urban meanings, through its exoticizing of urban others. This is significant in that the urban has become a metaphor for race and in a white supremacist culture that identifies race with being black, the urban becomes another way to signify the pleasures and danger of blackness in the city. But in exoticizing and play-ing with black popular culture mainstream white culture reconstructs race as ethnicity, while at the same time essentializing or naturalizing ethnicity through race. Cross and Keith in agreement observe that "ethnicity is celebrated in the collage of the exotic cultural pick-and-mix, while race remains taboo, and is anything but playful. But like all taboos, it remains ever present, even in the systemic silences and exclusions" (1993:8). In the context of gentrification or redevelopment, mainstream white consumer culture's exoticization of the city has meant the development of "white pleasure spaces," places where mainstream whites, in what were once poor black neighborhoods, indulge in the exotic consumption of black music, dance, sports, and fashion, with the security of police and electronic surveillance to guard against the dangerous blacks.

This chapter will address as a pedagogical process the transformation of black urban settlements to spaces of private consumption for mainstream whites, as well as the effects of this on black urban popular culture and consciousness. I will argue that the production of urban meaning is not simply dominated by mainstream white consumer culture, but rather, in an effort to make place, black popular culture reappropriates the dominant racialized and essentialized meanings of the urban. Such reappropriations are attempts by blacks to create an urban culture of resistance. I will also examine the contradictions of black popular culture regarding the production of urban meanings, particularly with respect to how racially essentialist meanings of the urban undermine the production of black public spaces, and therefore black solidarity. A pedagogy of black urban struggle, I will argue, must be tied to a black liberatory politics of the body. Although hooks and West do not address the effects of white supremacist culture's essentialized racial meanings in relation to the production of city space, they do express the pedagogical consequence of these meanings for how black people view their bodies:

> One of the things we are in great need of is a discourse that deals with the representation of the black

body. In most Black homes, across class, there is tremendous unease in relation to the body, nakedness, and the representation of blackness. Part of this comes from white supremacist discourse associating Black being with Black bodies, as if we have no minds, no intelligence, are only the sum total of our visible physicality, and therefore the issue of whether Black people actually like and love their bodies becomes a crucial thing. (1991:86)

Chapter Two

Black Cultural Identity,
White Consumer Culture,
and the Politics of Difference

I Got Nothin' To Lose Much To Gain
In My Brain I Got A Capitalist
migrain.
I Care Nothin 'bout You And That's
evident,
All I Live Is My Dope And Dead
presidents.
Sound Crazy? Well It Isn't.
The Ends Justify The Means That's
the System
I Learned That In School, Then I
dropped Out,
Hit The Street, Checked The Grip,
now I Got Clout.
I Had Nothin, And I Wanted It.
You Had Everything And You
flaunted It.

Turned The Needy Into The Greedy,
With Cocaine, My Success Came
speedy.
Got Me Twisted, Jammed Into A
paradox,
Every dollar I get another brotha'
drops.
Maybe that's the plan and I don't
understand,
Goddamn, you got me sinking in
quicksand.
But since I don't know and I ain't never
learned,
I gotta get paid, I got money to earn.
. . . Is this a nightmare, or the
American dream!

> —ICE-T, lyrics to *New Jack Hustler*

The legacy of slavery mediated with
Jim Crowism, second-class citizenship,
urbanization, all the different stages
and phases that black people have
been through from 1619 up to present,
are followed by the culture of con-
sumption that begins to become more
and more dominant between 1965 and
the present. This has produced what I
want to argue is the major challenge
presented to black America: the high-
est level of forms of self-destruction
known in black history.

> —Cornel West, "Philosophy and the
> Urban Underclass," 1992

Introduction

The above quotations by Cornel West and Ice-T speak to
the way in which mainstream white consumer culture

affects black cultural identity by transforming the public spaces of the black community into private spaces of consumption, into spaces where the market values of individualism, consumption, and competitiveness dominate. This is significant because in the mythology of the "new urbanism" representations of the "postmodern" city rely upon mainstream white supremacist images of blacks as both exotic and dangerous to construct consumer-oriented lifestyles. Cross and Keith note, "Ethnicity is celebrated in the collage of the exotic cultural pick-and-mix . . . the centrality of race to the configuration of the postmodern city, turns out on closer inspection not to be missing at all, unspoken" (1993:8). What this means is that we must look critically at the relationship between black cultural identity and white consumer culture. In doing so, we are able to shift the dialogue about the shattering of black civil society—black families, neighborhoods, schools, churches—away from the "culture of poverty" paradigms of liberal structuralists and cultural conservatives toward a focus on how white supremacist discourse regulates the formation of black cultural identity (West, 1991b). The importance of shifting the dialogue is that it refocuses the issue of the deterioration of black civil society in terms of how white supremacist beliefs and images—which permeate U.S. society—leave wounds and scars that attack on a daily basis black intelligence, ability, beauty, and character in both subtle and overt ways. Equally important is the need for a discourse that reveals how dominant paradigms limit the way blacks respond to their predicament in America. The question then becomes, how has black culture reincorporated and even appropriated the "negative" or "racist" imagery of the dominant culture, and how has this incorporation regulated black politics? In reference to this question, Cornel West in *Prophesy and Deliverance* writes,

> The two basic challenges presently confronting Afro-Americans are those of self-image and self-determination. The former is the perennial human

attempt to define who and what one is, the sem-
piternal issue of self-identity; the later is the political struggle to gain significant control over the
major institutions that regulate people's lives. These
challenges are abstractly distinguishable, yet con-
cretely inseparable. In other words, culture and politics must always be viewed in close relation to each
other. (1983:22)

It is these two basic issues that inform Manning
Marable's question: "Given the state of affairs, why aren't
Afro-Americans rioting in the streets? What is keeping a
check on black urban militancy, when the material and
social conditions which gave rise to the riots of the 1960s
are actually much worse today" (1992:14)? He responds
later to his question by saying, "The worst manifestation of oppression is that which is generated internally,
not externally" (1992:14). An example of this attitude
was seen in a recent news hour interview with a gang
member turned youth worker who commented with
respect to black homicide, "Nowadays people are much
more afraid of living than of dying." One manifestation of
this is what Cornel West describes as "walking
nihilism," a term which suggests "[l]ife without meaning, hope and love [that] breeds a cold hearted, mean-
spirited outlook that destroys both the individual and
others" (1991b:223).
    Supporting in a more general way West and Marable's
concern about "internalized racism" and its implication for
black urban resistance, in his essay "Towards a Theory of
Collective Action," Alberto Melucci asserts that "[i]n contemporary society we find an emerging awareness of the
capacity to act upon action itself—to intervene in our moti-
vational and biological structures. The social and individual
potential for action becomes itself the object of action"
(1989:33). Melucci is referring to the capacity of consumer
capitalism, in an age of new information systems and com-

munication technologies, to regulate identity and action through its capacity to produce and inscribe meanings in its commodities.

This is of particular concern given that white wealth and power control the electronic media. It exerts great influence over the production of popular culture and how we interpret racial difference. The major issue is that the ideology of white supremacy undergirds many of the assumptions and ideas of white mainstream culture. Related to this, popular culture has been one site in which mainstream white culture has been able to "provide an ideological framework of symbols, concepts, and images through which we understand, interpret, and represent racial difference" (Omi, 1989:114), even when we attempt to resist white supremacist stereotypes (Haymes, 1994).

The capacity to create what hooks calls "radical black subjectivities," which challenge and transform white supremacist domination when linked to political action, depends on blacks "critically deconstructing" white consumer culture and how it is implicated in their identity. Blacks therefore must learn to analyze how popular culture is constructed around a "politics of difference" or "politics of diversity." This means that blacks must consider the following:

1. that mainstream white culture's politics of difference reproduces white supremacist stereotypes, by making black culture a marker for racial difference, so that whites are deracialized and blacks are racialized;
2. that this particular construction of racial difference avoids dialogue about the issue of race and makes race the problem of blacks, not whites; and
3. that the cultural authority of the white mainstream culture constructs blacks as either exotic or dangerous by sexualizing their racial physical characteristics.

The implication is that black culture is viewed as either sexually provocative or pathological. Later, I will examine these issues in more detail, but for now I want to look at how "whiteness" in white consumer culture is politically parasitic on "blackness" for its self-definition, and along with this the consequences of "liberal integrationism" on black self-image and black self-determination.

Liberal Integrationism and White Consumer Culture

In addition to mystifying the political and property relations that perpetuate and maintain white hegemonic domination and privilege, "liberal integrationism" produces and regulates how blacks pedagogically take up their identity as blacks. That is, the ideology of "liberal integrationism" functions not only to reproduce market forces, but also "market mentalities," which in *Habits of the Heart* Robert Bellah associates with the "culture of consumption" of the white American middle class, who incidentally have been the benefactors and perpetuators of "consumer capitalism" since its global dominance. In addition to this Bellah argues that this "culture of consumption" has transformed the public spaces from a "community of memory" into "lifestyle enclaves" (1985).

The dominance of "liberal integrationism" as an ethical referent for black liberation and black freedom has had dire consequences for the social stability of black-controlled institutions. One reason is liberal integrationism's liberal humanist interpretation of race and ethnicity. The liberal interpretation of race and ethnicity has as its goal the achievement of a "democratic" color-blind society within the structures of consumer capitalism, or in the words of Martin Luther King, a society in which "[blacks] will not be judged by the color of their skin but by the content of their character." The assumed belief of King and other civil rights leaders was that there was a "common humanity" and that black people were really like white people. This belief effectively eliminated differences in history and culture between whites and blacks (West, 1991a).

Underlying the liberal humanist notion of a "common humanity" is the Eurocentric idea that, regardless of racial and ethnic differences, human beings are all the same because they are autonomous, rational individuals. But within a white culture of middle-class consumption, "market mentalities" dictate that individuality should be understood more in terms of what C. B. Macpherson called "possessive individualism." That is, individuality is conceptualized as "freedom from dependence on the wills of others, and freedom as a function of possession" (Macpherson, 1962:4).

Meanwhile, what is at stake is the relation of the individual to community, because as Macpherson writes, in the context of "possessive individualism [s]ociety becomes a lot of free equal individuals related to each other as proprietors of their own capacities and of what they have acquired by their exercise. Society consists of relations of exchange between proprietors" (1962:3). Therefore, within the cultural perimeters of a society organized around "white" consumption, everyday life is reduced to a commodity, to a market relation. The result of this is that market mentalities are created, and as West observes, "people think the only way to achieve is to get over on someone else, to treat people as if they were simply objects hindering or benefitting one's own advancement" (1991b:95).

The failure of black institutions to encourage interdependence can be attributed in part to the erosion of community, to the loss of understanding of the importance of mutual interdependence and communal living, and to the abandonment of faith in the ability to collectively shape the terms of our survival (hooks and West, 1991:52). It is the intrusion of white "consumer capitalism" into black life that has been responsible for the erosion of community and political solidarity. What is meant by "black life" is "everyday life" or what Henri Lefebvre refers to as "the dull routine, the ongoing go-to-work, pay-the-bills, homeward trudge of daily existence" (1990:vii). And although made to appear "natural" it is not, because what programs the routines of our everyday life is bureaucratically controlled consumption; the everyday has become an object of programming for consumer capitalism.

What does this mean for understanding the predicament of black people in America, particularly the ability of their social institutions to develop collective and critical consciousness, moral commitment, and courageous political engagement? Unfortunately, what has happened is that black institutions have lost their ethical commitment and vision, their sense of what ought to be, and consequently their ability to initiate what bell hooks and Cornel West describe as the process of "collective black self-recovery." In short, black institutions are in a period of crisis because they are unable to confront the despair, hopelessness, disappointment, alienation, fear, frustration, pain, and suffering of blacks resulting from what Cornel West refers to as the "existential crisis" of black Americans. In the words of bell hooks, black institutions and their leadership have lost the ability "to take pain, work with it, recycle it, and transform it so that it becomes a source of power" (hooks and West, 1991:8). The reason for this crisis in the black community is that the liberal integrationist ideology of the civil rights movement meant the incorporation of black Americans into a consumer culture. They have been integrated into a way of life where the market values of consumer capitalism such as individualism, materialism and competitiveness strongly influence how blacks experience everyday life.

Henri Lefebvre pointed out that the everyday has become a social practice because "the extension of capitalism goes all the way to the slightest details of ordinary life" (1990:79). He makes this observation because of the relationship between multinational corporations and the economy in producing consumer goods for everyday life. At this point, social needs and the everyday have been programmed by advertising and the media and are managed and administered by the huge investments of these corporations. This linked with the Keynesian welfare state has resulted in the further commodification and bureaucratization of social needs and the everyday through the provision of services like housing, health, education, and transportation. Therefore, the everyday has become controlled and manipulated, an object of social organization (Mouffe, 1988).

What this means is that in consumer capitalism the material objects of everyday life (furnishings, clothes, shelter, food, transportation, neighborhood, etc.), including leisure time, are regulated through bureaucratically controlled consumption or the rational planning of obsolescence by private corporations. Through planned obsolescence the material objects of everyday life are manipulated to make them less durable, so that needs become outdated and replaced by new needs, thereby manipulating desire. Besides calling this a "strategy of desire" Lefebvre refers to this as the "rationalized exploitation of everyday life" (1990:87). Behind this is the assertion that the concept of production involves not only the "making of things," but also the self-production of human beings. In this context production is equated with reproduction and reproduction with consumption. The point being that social order or the preservation of the societal arrangements in United States does not just rest on discipline in the workplace, at the site of production, but also must involve the organization of consumption in everyday life.

The "consumption ethic" more than the "work ethic" has become the basis of liberal integration. This is an important insight and shift because the high rates of black unemployment and underemployment have removed large numbers of blacks from the subjugation of workplace discipline. For the American working population in general, the deskilling of the labor process has resulted in subordinating the more humanist impulse (for example, self-realization and creativity) of the work ethic to the more puritanical, productivist ideology and technical logic (i.e., Taylorism, and Fordism) of business (Gorz, 1982). In order to contain workers' resentment and unrest against the "disciplinary regime of productivism" and integrate them into the main-stream of daily life, American business promoted the ideology of consumption (Ewen, 1976; Gorz, 1989). It is in this context that life at work, understood as drudgery, became the negation of life outside of work, the everyday, which consumer capitalism "colonized" and saturated with make-believe images and signs of a conspicuously wealthy lifestyle of leisure that Thorstein Veblen (1953) had equated with the "leisure class."

Before returning to how this has served to manage rest-less populations, I want to focus attention on how the identity of black Americans has been inscribed in the images and signs of white consumer culture. It is in this context of white hegemonic power and authority that black Americans have assumed a "market morality" in which self-understanding means living to consume. This in turn "creates a market culture where one's communal and political identity," West writes, "is shaped by the adoration and cultivation of images, celebrityhood, and visibility." He concludes that "this is fundamentally transforming [the] Black community in very ugly ways" (1991b:96). It is presumed that the ideological dominance of "consumption-ism" has regulated the way in which blacks comfort and transform their psychic pain and suffering. This illustrates the depth of black Americans' integration into white consumer culture.

More than the consumption of things, we consume the images and signs that those things are made to evoke. Or as Lefebvre observes, "Consumer goods are not only glori-fied by signs and 'good' in so far as they are signified; consumption is primarily related to these signs and not to the goods themselves" (1990:91). Another way of putting this is that the "value" of consumer goods has not only to do with market "supply and demand" or the "amount of nec-essary labor-time," as suggested by bourgeois and Marxist political economists, but also with how "commodities" are signified or given meaning, particularly in the context of consumer capitalism (Baudrillard, 1981).

This indicates that the meanings given to consumer goods have an endless referentiality and are different to different groups depending on their production and reception (Baudrillard, 1981). According to Stuart Hall, "Culture has ceased to be a decorative addendum to the "hard world" of production and things, the icing on the cake of the material world. The word is now as material as the world" (1990:129). He further elaborates that "[t]hrough design, technology and styling, 'aesthetics' has already penetrated the world of modern production. Through marketing, layout and style, the 'image' provides the mode of representation and fictional narrativisation of the body on which so much modern consumption depends" (1990:129). In short, modern capitalism is moving from the "exchange of commodities" to the "exchange of signs." Or, rather, the sign and the commodity are becoming a single, identical form, which Jean Baudrillard refers to as the "political economy of the sign" (1980:206).

One way to understand this move is to look at how the role of mass advertising has changed in relation to the politics of consumption. From the 1920s to the mid-1970s, mass advertising emerged alongside the standardization of mass consumption, which had arisen because of the high productivity of U.S. technology. Therefore, the major concern of this period was with the continual adjustment of mass consumption with rises in productivity. And, although worker's wages increased and the availability of personal credit increased, mass advertising, nonetheless, was one of the most important factors in stimulating consumer demand (Davis, 1986; Lipietz, 1987; Murray, 1990). Some refer to this period as "American Fordism," which was marked by the strategy of raising workers' wages to achieve a corresponding increase in overall demand. This strategy also aimed to counter radicalism and communism among workers, particularly in the 1930s and 1940s, by giving them a stake in the "American Dream" through a relatively high standard of living (Davis, 1986).

However, what distinguished the method of mass advertising during this period was its overriding emphasis on
price or social competitiveness. Because of product standardization, consumer goods produced by competing man-
ufacturers were thought to be basically the same, only differentiated by selling price. Therefore, during this period,
consumers were motivated to "keep up with the Joneses" by
accumulating the most durable goods (refrigerators, TVs,
washing machines, automobiles, stereos, and homes) at the
lowest prices. This period of advertising is characterized by
Frank Mort as "the sell 'em cheap, pile 'em high campaigns
of the 1960s and 1970s" (1990:168). Along with mass advertising the post-war economic growth was fueled by high
wages for the majority of the population—the industrial
white working class. For them, the American Dream
included a home in the suburbs, a car, and college for their
kids.

It is this materialistic ethos that Manning Marable
claims has undermined black consciousness and identity:
"One major factor in the demise of black consciousness and
identity was the materialism and greed inherent in the
existing American political economy and secular society.
By asking to be integrated into the system, blacks became
hostage to their own ideological demands" (1992a:21).
Marable's comment about the consequences of "materialism" in the black community, nevertheless, must be understood in the context of how mass advertising and consumption have changed since the transition away from American
Fordism.

The Transition from Fordism and the Politics of Consumption

With the tendential equalization of income and productivity levels—due in part to a dynamic wage system that
synchronized mass consumption with labor productivity—
there occured a parallel trend towards the "relative satura-

tion" of the consumer-durable markets (Davis, 1986:196). Mike Davis argues that this relative saturation, which contributed to stagflation in the mid to late 1970s, was responsible for the crisis in Fordism. The consumer-durable markets were the primary engines that coordinated the expansion of American consumer capitalism (Davis, 1989:195:201).

One major solution to this crisis, referred to as "neo-Fordism," was the state-led provision of higher standards of living, which involved the reorientation of public spending and taxation and expansion in the provision of public services and collective consumption (i.e., new income and welfare entitlements, health care, education, recreation, and urban development). However, unlike the strategy of Fordism, which sought to fuel demand by integrating the industrial working class via higher wages, neo-Fordism aimed, through an expanded welfare state, to fuel demand and economic growth by also integrating poor and working-class blacks into the American Dream, particularly in the aftermath of the urban rebellions in the 1960s.

However, since the election of Ronald Reagan in 1980, the neo-Fordist strategy has been blocked by an emerging (mostly new white) middle strata of salaried managers, professionals, new entrepreneurs, credentialed technicians, and rentiers whose survival has depended on the expansion of the service economy. Securing its survival has been due, in part, to its capacity to effectively mobilize politically (e.g., the New Right). In addition to its racist law and order politics and mobilizations to enact state legislation limiting property and income taxes, this new class after 1976 was also responsible for the suburban protests, which included the antibusing and educational back-to-basics movement and the rentier and landlord mobilizations against rent control and public housing (Davis, 1986).

Furthermore, the political project of this new class has been more hegemonic than the earlier backlash of the ethnic northern working class or the national Wallace movement. Indeed, as part of the leadership of the New Right, the new white middle class has been hegemonic since the 1980s in that it has succeeded in upwardly redistributing power and income by shifting tax burdens, privatizing public services, and dismantling obstacles to the exploitation of cheap labor. All of this has been combined with shifts in corporate investment from labor to financial and real estate markets. Therefore, it has been the post-Fordist strategy of the new white middle class that has fueled both the expansion of the service economy and their power and privilege within it.

This strategy has not only created a polarization of the "haves" and "have nots" in terms of labor market restructuring, but has also affected the consumer-goods market. For instance, in relation to the consumption side of the service economy, private capital has applied new technology and new production principles to retailing to make Fordism flexible. In an effort to counter the relative saturation in the consumer-goods market and curve stagflation, retailers developed information and supply systems that allowed them to order supplies to coincide with demand. In turn, this permitted retailers to trade the limits of the mass product for a market niche strategy. Whereas previously stores were restricted to carrying a few fast-selling items, a market niche strategy allowed retailers to carry a broad range of products, targeting new middle class households in particular (Murray, 1989:43-44).

A market niche approach involved the categorizing of the market by researchers according to the different lifestyles of consumers based on varied consumption patterns. Differences in lifestyle have mostly been categorized vertically to confirm status and class. Therefore, "instead of keeping up with the Joneses, there has been a move to be different from the Joneses" (Murray 1990:44). The argument is that through product differentiation the new white middle class has been able to consume "a style of life" that distinguishes them in terms of status. Barbara Ehrenreich sums this up nicely when she writes,

One of the unappealing features of 1950s-style mass marketed affluence, for a middle class point of view, was that it allowed for only "minute distinctions" between the middle class and those immediately below, the working class. One might have more and better, but "better" was not distinctively different: thicker carpets, a car with more options, museum prints rather than dime-store reproductions on the wall. In the eighties this problem was decisively resolved. The mass market disappeared and was replaced by two markets, which we know as "upscale" and "downscale." The change reflected the growing middle class zeal to distinguish itself from the less fortunate. (1989:228)

Related to the issue of middle-class status distinction is the role of advertising in suggesting atmosphere—a style of life—with a message which is "emotional" rather than rational or informational (Mort, 1990:168). "Color, sound and shape," Frank Mort observes, "are the things which mark out individuality, nudging [middle class white] consumers to identify with commodities through mood and association" (1989:168). This, however, must be understood in relation to how "style is a way that the human values, structures, and assumptions in a given society are aesthetically expressed and received" (Ewen, 1976:3).

Black Culture, White Identity, and the Cultural Politics of White Consumerism

With the importance "style" is given in advertising, "the act of consuming [has become] as much an act of imagination as a real act" (Lefebvre, 1990:90). In part, this points to the fact that "[i]n the commodification of language and culture, objects and images are torn free of their original referents and their meanings become a spectacle open to almost infinite translation"(Rutherford, 1990:11). One instance of this is the exotic preoccupation and consumption of black American popular culture by mainstream whites. Thus, in the act of consuming, white middle-class sensibilities, tastes, and lifestyles are predicated on consuming black images that have more to do with the white racist imagination. Jonathan Rutherford implies this when he says: "Otherness is sought after for its exchange value, its exoticism and the pleasure, thrills and adventures it can offer" (1990:11), creating a society where "the [white] middle class scavenges the earth for new experiences to be woven into a collective, touristic version of other people and other places" (MacCannell, 1989:13).

In fact, the sign of the "cultured" or the "civilized" attitude, Homi Bhabha writes, "is the ability to appreciate cultures in a kind of *musee imaginaire*; as though one should be able to collect and appreciate them." He continues: "Western connoisseurships is the capacity to understand and locate cultures in a universal time-frame that acknowledges their various historical and social context only eventually to transcend them and render them transparent" (1991:208). Thus, the likeness of white middle-class consumption to "tourism" provides some insight into how it views and regulates cultural difference. Dean MacCannell believes that for middle-class whites, tourism or "sightseeing is a ritual performed to the differentiation of society":

> Sightseeing is a kind of collective striving for a transcendence of the modern totality, a way of attempting to overcome the discontinuity of modernity, of incorporating its fragments into unified experiences. . . . This effort of the [white] middle to coordinate the differentiations of the world into a single ideology is intimately linked to its capacity to subordinate other people to its values, industry and future design. The [white] middle class is the most favored now because it has a transcendent consciousness. Tourism, I suggest, is an essential component of that consciousness. (1989:13)

It is through language and culture that middle-class whites, within the parameters of consumer capitalism, coordinate and contain cultural difference, while celebrating and consuming black culture (West, 1989:94). One way of understanding this contradiction is by looking at how white identity is constituted through the politics of language, discourse, and difference. This approach presents a departure from the Cartesian view of the subject, which has dominated modern discourse in the West (e.g., Liberal humanism).

According to the Cartesian view, the "self" or subject is a unified, integrated ego and as such a repository of consciousness and creativity" (Giroux, 1991:129). The presumption is that "the subject is constituted through the exercise of a rational and autonomous mode of understanding and knowing" (Giroux, 1991:129) outside the politics of language and discourse (West, 1983). In this Cartesian tenet, individual selves, subjects, or identities are able to perfectly replicate themselves as mirror images, thereby neglecting the mediating role that language plays in constituting identities and their representations. However, identity is not outside of representation, because we use language to describe ourselves. In the words of Stuart Hall, "[i]dentity is a narrative of the self; it's the story we tell about the self in order to know who we are" (1991:16).

It is in this context that middle-class white authority, through its institutional power and privilege within consumer capitalism, imposes structures of meaning on black narratives, consequently regulating how blacks come to know who they are as blacks. Nevertheless, the structures of meaning imposed that regulate the formation of black identity have more to do with how whites come to know who they are as whites. The point is that to understand the negative effects of white consumer culture on black culture, we must first recognize the historically specific ways that "whiteness" is a politically constructed category that is parasitic on "blackness." Thus as Stuart Hall comments, "[Whites] are racist not because they hate the blacks, but because they don't know who they are without blacks. They have to know who they are *not* in order to know who they are" (1991:16).

Within the logic of white supremacy difference is defined as the black Other. Black identity functions for white culture as a way to mark off difference and define what is *normal*. Richard Dyer supports this when he claims that in contemporary society power passes itself off as embodied in the normal as opposed to the superior. Furthermore, he says, "This is common to all forms of power, but it works in a peculiarly seductive way with whiteness, because of the way it seems rooted, in common-sense thought, in things other than ethnic difference" (1988:20). The argument is that racial and ethnic differences must be understood in relation to other Western Eurocentric discourses that define the conceptual meanings of white and black.

In Western culture, the concept of 'white' is represented in direct opposition to the concept of 'black.' As Winthrop Jordon indicates, "No other colors so clearly implied opposition, . . . no others were so frequently used to denote polarization" (1968:7). The positioning of white and black as polar opposites is significant because as Jacques Derrida argues, Western metaphysics has always privileged one term in a binary opposition over the other (Sarup, 1989:40-42). And in Eurocentric Western culture this has been consistent with the concepts of white and black. As Winthrop Jordan asserts, "White and black connoted purity and filthiness, virginity and sin, virtue and baseness, beauty and ugliness, beneficence and evil, God and the devil"(1968:7). What is important is how the concepts of white and black in dominant representations come to be naturally conflated as race and ethnic categories. And how does this function to reproduce white privilege and domination in ways that white people "colonize" the definition of normal?

One way to pursue this question is to pair the concepts of black and white with the idea of color. Hence, "black is always marked as a colour, and is always particularizing;

whereas white is not anything really, not an identity, not a particularizing quality, because it is everything—white is no colour because it is all colours" (Dyer, 1988:20). Thus within the binary logic, Eurocentric or white supremacist discourse conceals what to "blackness" is Other by making whiteness invisible. The process is one of racializing blackness while deracializing whiteness. Kobena Mercer (1988:32) agrees when he says, "Whiteness has secured universal consent to its hegemony as the norm by masking its coercive force with the invisibility that marks off the Other as all too visible—coloured."

To expose the invisibility of whiteness is to *unmake* race and ethnic difference as exclusive to blacks. Similarly, Henry Giroux argues that the discourse of white supremacy creates "the self delusion that the boundaries of racial inequality and ethnicity were always exclusively about the language, experience, and histories of the Other and had little to do with power relations at the core of its own cultural and political identity as the discourse of white authority" (1991:220). Therefore, to talk about the marginalization, oppression, and subordination of black identity, white identity must be made visible (Carby, 1986:39). But the difficulty lies in that whiteness itself is masked as a category. The "colorlessness" of whiteness secures white domination and privilege because white people do not see their own whiteness. This notion of white identity was confronted in the video *Being White*.

> Asked how they would define themselves, the white interviewees refer easily to gender, age, nationality or looks but never to ethnicity. Asked if they think of themselves as white, most say that they don't, though one or two speak of being "proud" or "comfortable" to be white. In an attempt to get some white people to explore what being white means, the video assembles a group to talk about it and it is here that the problem of white people's inability to see whiteness appears intractable. Subcategories of

whiteness (Irishness, Jewishness, Britishness) take over, so that the particularity of whiteness itself begins to disappear; then gradually, it seems almost inexorably, the participants settle in to talking with confidence about what they know; stereotypes of black people. (Dyer, 1988:46)

What is revealing here is that as whites move implicitly towards defining themselves as a universal norm and become elusive, they explicitly draw on black stereotypes. The idea is that for whites to have a self-perception as rational, ordered, and civilized, they have to construct a notion of irrationality, disorder, and uncivilized behavior (Young, 1992:193). It is in this context that black stereotypes serve as a referent for whites to construct their own identity.

Of interest here is how stereotypes through language situate or position us politically and ideologically in relation to each other. To say that we are discursively positioned implies that language dictates the rules that govern what can be said, what must remain unsaid, who can speak with authority, and who must listen. Of central concern here is the process of differentiation implicit in how we use language. The assumption is that we learn who we are by differentiating ourselves from each other. That is, in the context of a middle-class hegemonic white consumer culture, the use of language as well as its process of differentiation must be understood in relation to white fears and anxieties about their perceived loss of control and order (Young, 1992). For example, as the racial and ethnic landscape in the United States becomes more and more African, Latin, and Asian American, the certainty, or rootedness and centeredness, of white identity is disrupted and threatened by difference.

Fearful that this difference results in its dissolution, white identity invests the Other with its terror. This sense, "the threat of dissolution . . . ignites irrational hatred and hostility as [white identity] struggles to assert and secure its boundaries, that construct self from not self" (Rutherford,

1990:11). Whites repress their anxiety, their fear of losing control due to racial difference, by projecting that anxiety onto blacks. Sander Gilman, in *Difference and Pathology: Stereotypes of Sexuality, Race, and Madness*, believes that "[the] deep structure of [white people's] sense of self and the world is built upon the illusionary image of the world divided into two camps, "us" and "them." They are either "good" or "bad" (1985:17).

But to divide the world into two camps is to construct a crude mental representation of the world, or what Gilman refers to as stereotypes, which are manufactured when constructing difference as binary oppositions (Gilman, 1985:17; Young, 1992:196). When configured as bipolar opposites an imaginary line is drawn to create an illusion of absolute difference between the self and the Other. Jonathan Rutherford agrees with this view when he writes,

> Binarism operates in the same way as splitting and projection: the centre expels its anxieties, contradictions and irrationalities onto the subordinate term, filling it with the antithesis of its own identity; the Other, in its very alienness, simply mirrors and represents what is deeply familiar to the centre, but projected outside of itself. It is in these processes and representations of marginality that the violence, antagonisms and aversions which are at the core of the dominant discourses and identities become manifest—racism, homophobia, misogyny and class contempt are the products of this frontier. (1990:22)

In this context, the construction of difference and its relationship to stereotyping is particularly potent when associated with anatomical signs of difference, such as physiognomy and skin color (Gilman, 1985:25; Young, 1992:196). This means that in view of the "white gaze," the black body is seen as being pathological. Sander Gilman believes that "order and control are the antithesis of pathology. Restated, "Pathology is disorder and the loss of control, giving over the self to the forces that lie beyond the self" (1985:24). He further asserts that one major category with which pathology is often associated is human sexuality. And that in the "white racist imagination," the black body represents hypersexuality and consequently carries a pathological image that signifies threat and disorder:

> Based on Hottentot physiology it was deduced that the black female possessed not only a "primitive" sexual appetite but also the external signs of this temperament—"primitive" genitalia. Black men, of course, were empirically proven to be endowed with oversized, "primitive" sexual organs as well. Enlarged labia, big buttocks and monstrous penises loomed large in the nineteenth century scientist's imagination as fearsome signifiers, signifiers of an animal-like hypersexuality that was threatening in its force. (Bailey, 1988:29)

Black stereotypes, nonetheless, are not rigidly constituted but are constantly shifting from fearing to exoticizing and from hating to loving blacks. Even "the most negative stereotype," Gilman observes, "always has an overtly positive counterweight. As any image is shifted, all stereotypes shift. Thus stereotypes are inherently protean than rigid" (1985:18). Cameron Bailey believes that this combined fear and exoticizing of the black body has functioned as a powerful signifier in Hollywood films:

> Since the cavalry rode manfully across the crosscutting to save Lillian Gish from blackness in *Birth of a Nation*, since Barbara Apollonia Chalupiec became Pola Negri and took up a position as Hollywood's resident Other, black sexuality, indeed anything other than white sexuality, has been both a potent threat and a powerful attraction in American film. Adopting a centuries old signification system, Hollywood from its beginning linked racial difference to sexual danger. Danger, we saw, lurked in a

captial-O Other: sexual transgression became
Hollywood's darkest sin, and its surest box-office
draw. (1988:28)

This combined fear and fascination with black sexuality
rests on whites not being fully aware of how the maintenance of their authority, power, and privilege is perpetuated by their invisibility as whites. This invisibility sees
"whiteness" as the center, as the universal norm and transcendental consciousness that speaks for everyone, while
being itself everywhere and nowhere (Mercer, 1990:6).

Although not explicit, white people's expressed feelings of culturelessness hints at a self-perception of having
a transcendental consciousness. Perhaps this has something to do with Western societies' presumption that it
possesses "reason" rather then culture. An example of this
idea is Allan Bloom's statement: "What is most characteristic of the West is science, particularly understood as
the quest to know nature and the consequent denigration
of convention—i.e, culture or the West understood as a
culture—in favor of what is accessible to all men as men
through their common and distinctive faculty, reason"
(1987:38). So what is implied is that as the West, through
its "scientific reason," discovers or makes visible nature,
meaning dark-skinned people, it transcends the particu-
larism of its own culture, making itself invisible. Or, as
Renato Rosaldo in *Culture and Truth* argues, "As the other
becomes more culturally visible the [white] self becomes
correspondingly less" (1989:202). So much less, that white
invisibility contributes to feelings of emptiness, absence,
denial, or even a kind of death, and therefore a reliance on
black culture to provide their white identity with substance (Dyer, 1990).

For example, cultural theorists argue that the racial aesthetics of early films such as *Birth of a Nation* foreground
the use of black culture as a signifier or marker of exotica in
contemporary North American white avant-garde and mainstream films (Bailey, 1987:40; Talyor, 1991:29). Clyde Taylor

in his article "The Rebirth of the Aesthetic in Cinema" argues that in white American cinema black culture "is *not* worshiped for itself but for the transcendental values it is believed to represent" (1991:22).

He discusses how in *Birth of a Nation* D. W. Griffith used whites in blackface to exploit the emotional dynamics of white audiences. "Under the mask of racial and moral darkness, hidden desires could be exercised and indulged in public performance, even glamorized and applauded. The minstrel mechanism . . . is one instance in which the ideological masking of unspeakable knowledge requires an actual mask" (Taylor, 1991:22). In reference to North American avant-garde films bell hooks asserts that "[w]hile it is exciting to witness a pluralism that enables everyone to have access to the use of certain imagery, we must not ignore the consequence when images are manipulated to appear 'different' while reinforcing stereotypes and oppressive structures of domination" (1991:171).

The implication behind the black-as-exotic stereotypes is that the black is more primitive or animal like. Cameron Bailey argues that within North American film, "the predominant physical stereotypes of blacks still hold currency—bulging eyes, thick lips, wide noses, enlarged sexual organs—turn the black into a rampaging figure of excess sensuality" (1988:13). These physical stereotypes suggest that the blacks' senses admit more than is "tasteful"; they are in bad taste because they are so obvious. The blacks' senses, in the white paradigm, consume too much" (Bailey, 1988:13). Yet, still within this paradigm, there is a complex fusion of desire and aversion, projection and concealment. Cornel West implies the same: "Given the European and Euro-American identification of Africans and African Americans with sexual licentiousness, libertinism, and liberation, black music became both a symbol and facilitator of white sexual freedom" (1989:95).

Black culture is therefore seen as providing substance or "life" to white identity, which defines itself as restrained, transparent, and neutral, and therefore lifeless. According to

Dyer, the desire to possess the Other is derived from the Eurocentric belief that nonwhite cultures are more "natural" than whites, and therefore represent "life":

> Life here tends to mean the body, the emotions, sensuality and spirituality; it is usually explicitly counterposed to the mind and the intellect, with the implication that white people's over-investment in the cerebral is cutting them off from life and leading them to crush the life out of others and out of nature itself. The implicit counterposition is, of course, "death." (Dyer, 1988:56)

In other words, the white middle-class culture of consumption has much to do with the consumption of black culture, which in the white imagination is a signifier of "life," but one in which white values, experiences, and history have cultural currency. Nevertheless, white culture's exotic interest in black culture has served as a healthy critique of the mechanistic, puritanical, utilitarian, and productivist aspects of modern life. This implies that to some degree black culture has provided the white subject with an oppositional identity. In reference to this Kobena Mercer asserts that "the logic of reversal that overvalorizes an identification with racial otherness is also profoundly expressive of a disaffiliation from dominant self-images, a kind of strategic self-othering." He concludes: "From noble savages to painterly primitives, the trope of the White Negro encodes an antagonistic subject position on the part of the white subject in relation to the normative codes of his or her own society."

Recognizing white culture's exotic interests in black music, dance, style, fashion, and linguistic innovation, consumer capitalism has played a pivotal role in the commodification of black culture in order to expand its middle-class white luxury consumer market. Except what has been commodified has not been black culture per se, but the sexualized exotic and primitivistic images and signs it evokes in the imagination of whites; henceforth, stereotypical black images and signs are inscribed in and on middle-class white American popular music, films, dance, television, styles, fashions, advertising, and magazines. Through the luxury consumer market, middle-class whites can purchase "a style of life" that permits them to imaginarily indulge in the exotic and sensual, in which black cultural productions are the signifiers.

While consumer capitalism claims that through luxury products white middle class consumers gain access to "new" kinds of erotic experiences, its commodification of black culture has been about the "reification" or "fetishizing" of black cultural practices, practices that according to Cornel West "have primarily focused on performance and pageantry, style and spectacle in music, sermons, and certain sports" (1989:92). Insofar as the "exchange-value" of white consumer goods is "determined" by black signifiers, the joining of black culture and consumer goods as a single, identical form has resulted in a separation of black cultural practices from the historical and social circumstances that gave them life (West, 1989:87-96; Baudrillard, 1981:204-12). The circumstances that bore black cultural practices arose from a reality historically constructed through white supremacist practices; a reality marked by black insecurity and real necessity. Reality became infused in the strategies and styles of black cultural practices that Cornel West characterizes as kinetic orality, passionate physicality, and combative spirituality:

> By kinetic orality, I mean dynamic repetitive and energetic rhetorical styles that form communities, e.g., antiphonal styles and linguistic innovations that accent fluid, improvisational identities and that promote survival at almost any cost. By passionate physicality, I mean bodily stylizations of the world, syncopations and polyrhythms that assert one's somebodiness in a society in which one's body has no public worth, only economic value as a laboring metabolism. And by combative spirituality, I mean a

sense of historical patience, subversive joy, and daily
perseverance in a apparently hopeless and meaningless historical situation. (1989:93)

The commodification of black cultural practices
involves this transformation into signifiers, absent of historical references to black life and absent of signification
other than making luxury consumer goods pleasurable to
middle-class whites. This stripping of history and significance from black culture has reduced it to a simulacrum, or
a copy without any original. This process allows for black
culture to be re-inscribed into white fantasies about black
sexuality, therefore reducing black cultural practices to performance, and performance to the black body's imagined
"natural" endowments.

Implied in this view is that blacks are primitive or ani-
mal-like, evoking images of sexual deviancy and danger
that in turn associate the black body with disease. As
Gilman elaborates: "It is specifically the physiology of the
blacks which predisposes them to mental illness. Here the
association of blackness and madness is made incontro-
vertible. An uncommon potential for madness is inherent
in the nature of the black" (1985:139). Therefore, at the
same time that the black body serves as a transcendental
signifier for the sexual fantasies and envy of white people,
nonetheless, it is also repulsive to the white gaze and is
seen as a threat. This is evident in white people's fears surrounding interracial sexual relationships, anxieties that
"link back to the old idea that blood varies from 'race' to
'race' and that mixing those bloods is undesirable" (Young,
1992:197).

Thus, within the context of postFordist consumer capitalism, middle-class white consumption has in part recon-
firgured the cultural politics of race in such a way that
"racism has acquired an explicitly cultural rather then biological inflection" (Gilroy, 1990:266). In other words, the
culturalism of the "new racism" is "without any overt reference to either race itself or the biological notions of dif-

ference that dominated the modern scientific racism of the nineteenth century" (Gilroy, 1990:266). For example, Paul Gilroy states:

> Culture is conceived along ethnically absolute lines, not as something intrinsically fluid, changing, unstable, and dynamic, but as a fixed property of social groups rather than a relational field in which they encounter one another and live out social, historical relationships. When culture is brought into contact with race it is transformed into a pseudobiological property of communal life. (1991:267)

Black Cultural Identity, Black History, and White Consumer Culture

The question at hand, however, is in what way has white consumer culture affected black cultural identity? In exploring this question, Malcolm X reminded us of the close relationship of black cultural identity to history and black history to social movement: "The greatest mistake of the movement has been trying to organize a sleeping people. . . . You have to wake the people up first to their humanity and to their heritage. Then you'll get action" (Epps, 1991:99). He also said, "History is a people's memory, and without a memory man is demoted to the lower animal" (Epps, 1991:43).

Both remarks provide a context for understanding the effects of white consumer culture on black cultural identity, particularly in terms of how it has limited the possibilities for blacks to develop countermemories and counternarratives that highlight, in particular, their past resistance to subjugation and oppression. Yet, this claim does not suggest that the close connection of black identity to the past is rooted in some "logocentric" view of black history that reduces the recalling of history to some transcendental timeless search for meaning or truth. Rather, the recalling of

black history is not about nostalgia but about a "re-evalua-
tion of and a dialogue with the past in the light of the present" (Hutcheon, 1989:19). This has been referred to as "the
presence of the past or maybe its "present-ification"
(Hassan, 1983). Therefore, situating the recalling of history
in terms of re-evaluating the present does not deny the existence of the past but questions whether we can ever know
that past other than through its textualized remains
(Hutcheon, 1989:19).

This observation implies that "culture" is constitutive
of the way we come to interpret our own histories through
"maps of meaning." In other words, culture shapes and
structures the social relations of a group as well as how
those shapes are experienced, understood, and interpreted
(Hall and Jefferson, 1976:11). Or, as Peter McLaren summarizes, "The term culture signif[ies] the particular ways in
which a social group lives out and makes sense of its given
circumstances and conditions of life" (1989:101). Raymond
Williams in *Marxism and Literature* has drawn similar con-
clusions about the relationship of culture to everyday life.
Williams's concept 'structure of feeling,' is central to understanding this relationship. He uses structure of feeling to
denote that the meanings and values we use to make sense
of our circumstances and conditions of life are actively lived
and felt. What this means is that consciousness and relationships have affective elements and that culture is not
about "feeling against thought, but thought as felt and feeling as thought" (Williams, 1977:132). And while institutions, belief systems, and social relations embody culture,
they cannot be seen as separate from how we actively live
and experience meanings and values.

It is in this context that black culture shapes how black
people come to interpret, understand, and experience their
predicament in America. Moreover, while the "political and
economic avenues have usually been blocked, specific cultural arenas become the space wherein black resistance is
channelled" (West, 1989:94). For example, Houston Baker,
Jr., argues that the distinctiveness of black American culture

is its vernacular expression that draws on the everyday life of poor and working-class black people (1984), an everyday life shaped by what Cornel West terms "thick" forms of oppression, like economic exploitation, state repression, or bureaucratic domination (1988:271). It is in their vernacular expressions in the form of music and speech that black people acknowledge "the ragged edges of the real, of necessity, not being able to eat, not having shelter, not having health care (West, 1988:271), "a reality they cannot *not* know, a reality historically constructed by white supremacist practices" (West, 1988:271; West, 1989:93).

In agreement with the theoreticians of the Black Arts movement of the 1960s, Houston Baker in *Blues, Ideology, and Afro-American Literature* argues that, in the context of the black condition and black cultural expression, the black vernacular functions as an "emotional referent" and "experimental category" that affords black people the space to confront and creatively deal with their psychic pain and suffering in America. But what is it that constitutes the black vernacular or the day-to-day conversations of black people that when infused in their music, dance, and speech strikes an "emotional cord"? Bell hooks argues that it has to do with how whiteness is represented in the "black imagination."

As a reaction to white stereotypes of blacks, bell hooks points out that black stereotypes of whiteness, which she describes as "evoking a simplistic and essentialists 'us' and 'them' dichotomy" where "blacks become synonymous with 'goodness' and whites with 'evil,'" are but one form of representing whiteness in the black imagination. Instead, she offers another representation of whiteness that "emerges as a response to the traumatic pain and anguish that remains as a consequence of white racist domination" (1992:341). She further argues that it is this traumatic pain and anguish that informs and shapes the "black gaze" or how blacks "see whiteness" (1992:341). This psychic state, hooks asserts, disrupts the fantasy in which blacks were socialized to believe that "whiteness represents goodness and all that is benign and nonthreatening" (1992:340). In place of this, whiteness in the black imagination is represented "as the terrible, the terrifying and the terrorizing" (hooks, 1992).

To better understand the association of whiteness with terror in the black imagination, hooks uses the concept of 'travel.' However, she distinguishes it from its conventional use wherein it is equivalent to play, to adventure, to tourism, all those things largely associated with the leisurely activities of middle-class whites. According to hooks, from the standpoint of blacks, to travel is to encounter the terror of white racist domination: police harassment, imprisonment, economic exploitation, hopelessness, and hunger and to confront that terror by journeying into the past and remembering the Middle Passage, enslavement, Jim Crow, and the mass migration of southern blacks to northern cities in the early part of the twentieth century.

Hooks elaborates that this journey for black folks is about "reconstructing an archeology of memory to help make sense of present locations" and that it is the remembering and telling of that history that makes possible what she calls "political self-recovery" (1991:343-45). This is what Michel Foucault meant when he said that memory is a site of resistance, that the process of remembering can serve as a practice which "transforms history from a judgement on the past in the name of a present truth to a counter-memory that combats our current modes of truth and justice, helping us to understand and change the present by placing it in a new relation to the past" (cited in hooks, 1992:344). So it was in the vernacular expressions or the day-to-day conversations of poor and working-class blacks that the process of remembering, when infused with their music and speech, allowed them to re-evaluate the present with the past while striking an "emotional cord" that inspired them to collectively struggle against white supremacist domination in the the 1960s and early 1970s.

Since that time, racial integration has had dire consequences in terms of the ability of blacks to create, out of their own cultural traditions and historical circumstances, a countermemory. One reason is because white consumer culture has "colonized" and is "parasitic" on black culture for the creation of "new experiences" for mostly middle-class white consumers through the commodification of black culture. In the aforementioned discussion of consumer capitalism and white consumer culture, I argued that the commodification of black culture has in part resulted in its reification and consequent detachment from any historical referent pertaining to black life. This has particularly been the case for black popular "middle-class" music, whose success in the recent past stems from its crossover to a principally white middle-class audience. West adds too that in "absolute terms, its domain has expanded because the black audience of middle class origin has also expanded" (1988:279). Moreover, the popular music of "middle-class" blacks distances itself from the expressive cultural practices of poor and working-class blacks, from the African polyrhythms and syncopation of the street in the day-to-day conversations about the pain and anguish of being terrorized by white people.

This distancing has to do with how the black middle-class diffuses the representation of whiteness as terror in the black imagination, so that it can forget the historical anguish of black people (hooks, 1992:335). This is further complicated by the anxieties of middle-class blacks steming from their sense of double consciousness—"namely their own crisis of identity, agency and audience—caught between a quest for White approval and acceptance and an endeavor to overcome the internalized association of Blackness with inferiority" (West, 1991a:28). The vernacular, expressive culture of the "black masses" contradicts the belief of privileged black folks, though at times critical, that America is destined to actualize its ideals of Liberal pluralism and that "mainstream culture" is an embodiment of those ideals (Baker, 1984:69). Working to assimilate into the "mainstream," middle-class blacks and their cultural expressions are mostly directed towards making the "mainstream culture" accountable to its own ideals of pluralism. Notwithstanding this effort, middle-class blacks fail to examine the manner in which white supremacist ideologies are able to regulate how race and ethnic difference get taken up in a supposedly pluralistic but also white consumer society.

Furthermore, in their aspiration to assimilate into a white-dominated consumer culture that regulates how blackness is represented in the imaginations of whites, the cultural productions of middle-class blacks become overwhelmingly directed towards trying to "salvage the denigrated image of blacks in the white American imagination" (Wallace, 1990:1). The manner in which this usually has been perceived is in terms of "positive" versus "negative" images. Michele Wallace in *Invisibility Blues* warns that this binary opposition of negative versus positive images results not in blacks challenging white supremacy, but in their collaborating with it. She argues that "since racism or the widespread conviction that blacks are morally and/or intellectually inferior, defines the 'commonsense' perception of blacks, a positive/negative image cultural formula means that the goal of cultural production becomes simply to reverse these already existing assumptions" (1990:1).

Wallace illustrates this with the example of the "Cosby Show" where blacks are shown as characters possessing the positive attributes of white culture (1991:2). These attributes are associated with being rational, ordered and civilized, all of which in the white imagination imply the absence of culture, the absence of life, and therefore this absense of emotion, sensuality, and spirituality. Therefore, in their effort to respond to white supremacy by representing themselves as "rational" and "civilized," middle-class blacks experience a sense of culturelessness, because like middle-class whites, they associate having culture with being black and poor. Signithia Fordham argues that for well-to-do blacks, "the practice of becoming raceless appears to have emerged as a strategy both to circumvent the stigma attached to being black, and to achieve vertical mobility"

(1988:58). In this sense, whiteness is treated as representing achievement, hard work, and control, and blackness is associated with pleasure and desire, suggesting disorder and laziness.

The consequence of this is that many of the same things that signify pleasure and desire in the white imagination, particularly in white consumer culture, do the same for well-to-do blacks, by providing images and signs that associate the expressive culture of the "black masses" with being sexually exotic and primitivistic. So it is in the context of a white consumer culture dominated by white supremacist images and beliefs that middle-class blacks, through their commercialized consumption of black culture, acknowledge or fulfill their emotional needs and longings. Referring to the Cosby show, Wallace says:

> Culture is reduced to a style of consumption that offers up, say, expensive, exotic-looking handknit sweaters, or a brief scene of the Cosbys at a jazz club where a black women is singing, rather than any concrete or complex textualization of cultural difference. Indeed the show seems to suggest, in its occasional use of Asians and Latinos as well as blacks, that no one is ultimately different, since culture is something you can buy at Bloomingdales, a kind of wardrobe or a form of entertainment. (1990:2)

The commercialization and consequent dehistorizing of black expressive culture, which in turn fostered a loss of "historical memory," has created what Cornel West describes as an "existential crisis" especially among well-to-do blacks. This has to do with them not knowing who they are, not having any historical memory from which to evaluate their present predicament. Without this sense of "historical memory," life becomes meaningless, leading middle-class blacks to turn to privatism and consumerism as a form of therapeutic release. This is further complicated by their "deep-seated anxiety and insecurity over their ability to be fully recognized and accepted by and into the main-

stream American middle class" (hooks and West, 1991:42).
In other words, to regain feelings of self-worth, the black
middle-class has dealt with a white supremacist assault on
black intelligence, black ability, black beauty, and black
character through class competition and material possession (hooks and West, 1991:98). This is particularly the case
in a society that falsely believes that goods function as an
equalizer and that there is opportunity through consumer
choice (hooks and West, 1991:98). For middle-class blacks
consumer choice has meant the opportunity to participate
in "upscale" white consumer markets, allowing them to
conspicuously draw status distinctions between themselves
and the rest of the black community.

Cornel West concludes that the integration of middle-
class blacks into white consumer culture has also produced
a "spiritual crisis" where selfishness, me-ness and egocen-
tricity are becoming the norm. One reason for this is that
religious faith is no longer linked with solidarity to the poor,
but rather with notions of progress and self-betterment.
This he argues has eroded the black middle-class's sense of
service, risk, and sacrifice to the black community.
Moreover, the erosion of risk and sacrifice can particularly
be seen in the way middle-class blacks censor the development of a certain kind of black cultural criticism. This is
due to their hunger for status, which is linked to their deep-
seated anxiety and insecurity regarding white approval. He
continues to say that although in the past their service ethic
had been petty bourgeois in form, middle-class blacks were
at least accountable to others in the community and would
put the needs of others in the community alongside their
own.

Poor and working-class blacks have also been negatively
affected by the hegemonic dominance of white consumer
culture. Their response to white supremacist stereotypes
has also been within the binary logic of negative versus positive images. However, what is different and at some level
empowering about the cultural politics of poor and working-
class blacks is that rather than associate positive images

with white culture, the "negative" or "racist" imagery of the dominant culture is reinterpreted as positive attributes of black culture (Wallace, 1990:2). Nevertheless, white supremacist discourse still dictates how blacks respond to stereotypes. The connotation of blackness with negative images and whiteness with positive ones is simply reversed, thus and the binary logic that informs the dominant discourse remains. Henry Louis Gates calls this "signifying," a term used to identify the reversal of white culture as the basis for the critical signification of black culture.

Part of this process involves what Elliott Butler-Evans describes as a "politics of self-fashioning" a term he uses to denote "the construction of a self that is different from, and removed from, a hostile Other" (1989:23). In this context, black self-image is largely generated by constructing whites as "alien and hostile Others." Undergirding this construction is the motive to displace white cultural authority by an oppositional black consciousness (Butler-Evans, 1989:24). This displacement entails a "symbolic inversion," a situation of inverting white culture to construct new definitions of blackness, creating counternarratives that generate alternative representations of black life.

One such counternarrative is "black nationalism." Its basic premise is that any kind of black oppositional culture and politics must be grounded in the expressive vernacular culture of the "black masses." From the perspective of white culture, black expressive culture is considered primitive because it is perceived as emotional and irrational, and anything emotional in Western discourse is associated with nature. However, black nationalism's rootedness in the "expressive" culture of the "masses" has allowed it to operate as a counternarrative by inverting and critically reinterpreting the meaning of emotion as it relates to constructing new definitions of blackness. For black nationalists, emotion and blackness are understood in terms of an "inner life" or "spirituality," whose formation is the result of an array of historically conditioned values and cultural codes. Moreover, these values and cultural codes allow blacks as a "community" or "reference public" to judge normatively what constitutes their inner life or spirituality.

In this vein, Larry Neal, a black cultural worker in the Black Arts movement of the 1960s, argues that the "ethos of the blues" is infused with the values and cultural codes that construct "black emotion," and henceforth blackness. He begins by asserting that the "blues are basically defiant in their attitude towards life" (1989:108). What Neal means is that the blues "are the expression of the larger will to survive—to feel life in one's innermost being, even though it takes place in an oppressive political context" (1989:108). For him, "the blues are primarily the expression of a post-slavery view of the world," referring to slavery's tendency to destroy the individual's sense of being a "person with particular needs and a particular style or manner of doing things" (1989:108, 112). Under slavery "every aspect of one's life is controlled from the outside by others, the sense of one's individual body is diminished" (1989:112). Neal concludes, that "the intensely personal quality of the blues is a direct result of freeing the individual personality which was held in check by slavery" (1989:112). Furthermore, because slavery was about white control and domination of the black body, the blues linked the emancipation of the individual black personality to a "politics of the flesh." The blues' "politics of the flesh" played a crucial role in affirming black humanity during the era of American industrialization. This assertion calls to mind Antonio Gramsci's comments regarding American Fordism: "The new type of man demanded by the rationalization of production and work cannot be developed until the sexual instinct has been suitably regulated and until it too has been rationalized" (1988:282). Therefore, the explicitly sexual content of the blues can be understood as a symbolic effort to free the black body and personality from white control and domination: "The blues are not concerned with middle class morality, black or white. That is because the audience that they address is forced to comfort the world of the flesh: the body is real, the source of much joy and pain. . . . The blues sing the joys and pain of the world of flesh, while pop songs of America rehash the dullness of a dying society" (Neal, 1988:114). In short, the blues are about black people experiencing slavery and surviving it and their "defiant attitude" that they will never be anybody's slave again.

It is this same attitude that is found in the rap music of inner-city black youth such as Public Enemy, Salt-N-Pepa, Roxanna Shante, Kurtis Blow, NWA, and Jungle Brother. It is an attitude that defies the control of their young black bodies through the terror of white hegemonic authority, an attitude not only reflected in their lyrics and musical forms, but also in their "crew names" like "Niggers with an Attitude." Moreover, like blues, jazz, and rhythm and blues, rap music's attitude embodies anti-Capitalist themes that can be traced directly or indirectly to the formative years of slavery. However, these themes represent thin forms of opposition. Quoting Cornel West:

> It is oppositional, but there are different levels of oppositionality. There's what we call "thin" opposition, and then there's "thick" opposition. Thin opposition is a critique of American society that does not talk about the need for a redistribution of wealth, resources, and power. Thick opposition is an attempt to call into question the prevailing maldistribution of wealth in this society. Thin opposition is important, but is not sufficient. And Black cultural influence has played a role in that thin opposition. Just affirming the humanity of Black People in America is still, in many instances, a subversive act. Yet, "thick" opposition is rarely put forward openly in Black culture. (1991:39)

These same themes Paul Gilroy argues amount to a critique of productivism—an ideology that makes capitalist economic growth a precondition for human freedom—that sees wage work itself as a form of servitude:

At best, [wage work] is viewed as a necessary evil and is sharply counterposed to the more authentic freedoms that can only be enjoyed in nonwork time. *The black body is here celebrated as an instrument of pleasure rather than an instrument of labor* [my emphasis]. The nighttime becomes the right time, and the space allocated for recovery and recuperation is assertively and provocatively occupied by the pursuit of leisure and pleasure. (1990:274)

Rap music also addresses the racist law-and-order politics of the Capitalist state, particularly the outright illegality and brutality of its policing of black bodies. Rappers see this brutality as denying blacks their status as legal subjects, reminding listeners that again "we" are being reduced to the status of slaves. Another theme that rap music concentrates on is the importance of history understood as a discontinuous process of struggle. It is a response to the way racism works by suppressing "the historical dimensions of black life offering a mode of existence locked permanently into a recurrent present where social existence is confined to the roles of being either a problem or a victim" (Gilroy, 1991:274).

However, the major weakness of rap music is that history is mostly recovered in the form of icons. And in most cases the historical icons are images of black men, thus fostering the false notion that black liberation has nothing to do with the specificity of black women's oppression. Another related concern is its phallocentrism, how black men in their efforts to resist racist domination unquestioningly invert white supremacist stereotypes of their bodies into an oppositonal culture that in fact demeans the bodies and personalities of both black women and black men. Denied access to the material privileges because of their race black men have found other ways to construct their masculine identities. The particular black male identities they construct dominate women in other ways. Unlike the patriarchal culture of mainstream white men, black males tend to rely much more on phallocentric models, in which masculine status depends solely on the penis. Bell hooks states: "With the emergence of a fierce phallocentrism, a man was no longer a man because he provided care for his family, he was a man simply because he had a penis. Furthermore, his ability to use that penis in the arena of sexual conquests could bring him as much status as being a wage earner and provider" (1993:94). Also problematic is the black neo-nationalist tendency to view black culture homogeneous and monolithic. By not understanding this, black nationalism collaborates with perpetuating the white supremacist stereotype that "blacks are all the same" and that language and discourse have nothing to do with the construction of blackness. In other words, what is perpetuated is an essentialist notion of blackness.

Furthermore, in rap music the politics of black nationalism gets played out through popular icons without any serious effort to recover the "historical context in which these icons emerged" (hooks and West, 1991:94). Moreover, the revival of black nationalism, particularly within the cultural productions of black youth, is symptomatic of a need for community and all of its meaning: primordial bonding, support, sustenance, projection of a future, and, of course, preservation of hope"(hooks and West, 1991:94). Nevertheless, the sort of black neo-nationalism being expressed evokes icons "without a sense of what kind of struggle must take place in order to carry out the mission of those icons" (hooks and West, 1991:95). In a sense, historical icons have become "commodities" whose images we buy and consume to feign or foster resistance: "The crucial issue for us is what are we going to do? Not how are we going to look, or what political slogan are we going to wear, but what forms of substantive struggle are we going to engage with our minds and bodies" (hooks and West, 1991:95).

Bell hooks argues that the playing out of black struggle and black liberation through popular icons is only indicative of "a real loss of sense of what to do" (hooks and West, 1991:95). She further asserts that "to be a people without an immediate sense of direction aggravates already present feelings of powerlessness" (hooks and West, 1991:95). What she is pointing to is how the hegemonic dominance of middle-class white consumer culture has lead to the collapse of structures of meaning and feeling in the black community. In part, this has to do with how white consumer culture has commodified black culture, reified it, disconnected it from its historical context, and used it for its own hedonistic purposes. Thus, white consumer culture has contributed immensely to feelings of meaninglessness in the black urban communities.

To live without meaning contributes to feelings of hopelessness. This is particularly the case for the large number of blacks who live in poverty-ridden urban neighborhoods, neighborhoods whose social formation is largely due to the expansion of a service economy fueled by the expensive lifestyles of middle class white consumers. In addition, with the breakdown of black civil society, blacks have become addicted to the stimulations of a consumer culture that makes its profits by degrading black bodies and personalities. In other words, to deal with the pain and anguish of white terror that wounds our pride and self-esteem we have now turned to the "luxury goods" of white consumer culture. This has gotten so serious that poor and working-class black youth now murder one another in pursuit of the right status symbol, such as a pair of sneakers. In the words of Anthony Parker, "Young blacks rarely recognize each other as brothers and sisters, or as comrades in the struggle. We're now competitors, relating to each other out of fear and mistrust" (cited in Marable, 1992a:21).

So, how must black cultural workers address poor and working-class black urban communities so their pain and anguish do not become channeled into self-destructive activity, but rather into meaningful collective resistance? For one thing, black cultural workers must develop a pedagogy of black urban resistance, which will be discussed in more detail later. For now, it will suffice to say that such a pedagogy must provide the context for urban blacks to critically engage their own cultural productions through the recovery of their history, but in ways that allow them to create a countermemory and culture of resistance. Nevertheless, in being urban-based, contemporary popular black culture must be understood in relationship to the historical-political-social formation of black urban settlements. In this way, the development of a culture of resistance must be tied to the formation of black cultural identity, recognizing how it associates with and organizes around territory. It is this relationship to which I now turn.

Chapter Three

Black Civil Society and the Politics of Urban Space

Historical Overview of Blacks in the City

David M. Hummon argues that the city in the American imagination has historically represented a "liberal place, where people are aware, open-minded, and particularly tolerant of social diversity" (1990:80). This image of city life was also related to the humanist ideas of the Enlightment, which viewed "the city as a place where the privacy of the individual is respected" and believed that it enhanced "personal freedom" (1990:80). According to John Jefferies, the Enlightenment ideals were "the inherent capacity of any individual to reason [his or her] way through a task, including the quest for personal fortune" and the Democratic notion that "all citizens have the opportunity to pursue any goals within reason, which could supposedly be actualized in the city" (1992:157). All of this pointed to the city as a place of expanded opportunity (Hummon, 1990:77), as a place of fair play where personal and societal progress was there for the asking (Jefferies, 1990:157). This was the romantic view of the "bourgeois city," a view that hid the harsh realities and predatory ethics of city life by merging free-market ideology with the Englightment's humanist concept of the self-determined individual, permitting the notion of personal fortune and progress to be defined around the making of profit, at all costs:

> In the American case, . . . cities are historical testimony to the perverse spatial offspring conceived and nurtured by the marriage of laissez-faire capitalism and those democratic principles that valorize the individual. Consider the behavior and conditions routinely rationalized in the name of profit, personal financial gain, or, what came to be synonymous— the hustle and bustle of the city: income generated by deliberately preying on and/or betraying family members, friends, and strangers; the unfettered destruction of the natural landscape and the pollution of the air and water; the construction and corruption of local law based on innumerable forms of privilege; high concentration of abject poverty and unprecedented personal wealth; the intractable commodification of space; and the constant redefinition of ultimately contradictory and conflicting designations of the public and private spheres. (Jefferies, 1993:158)

For the masses of black Americans that migrated from the urban and rural south to northern cities, during the "Great Black Migrations" of the early and mid-twentieth century, the Enlightment image of the city, the place of personal opportunity, fortune, and advancement was seldom, or if ever, realized through America's mainstream institutions. Nevertheless, the desire for a better life than the one in the South encouraged many southern blacks to migrate to the North in hopes of stable, well-paid employment. Richard Wright, in the introduction to St. Clair Drake and Horace

Cayton's *Black Metropolis*, notes that like whites, blacks too envision the city, in this case Chicago, as a place of great opportunity: "So, too, when the Negro, responding to the cultural hopes of his time, leaves the South and comes to the cold, industrial North, he is acting upon the same impulses that made them of the West great. The Negro can do no less; he shares all of the glorious hopes of the West, all of its anxieties, its corruptions, its psychological maladies" (1945:xxv). In an August 1917 letter to the editor of a black newspaper, *Dallas Express*, a writer sees the migration of blacks to the North and foreign immigration as similar: "And the Negro's motives for migrating North are but natural and they are similar to those which incite the foreigner to immigrate to America—the Negro is simply seeking to better his condition" (Adero, 1993:xix).

Some of the main reasons blacks left the South were "injustice in the courts, unrest, lack of privileges, denial of the right to vote, bad treatment, oppression, segregation or lynching, the relatively low wages paid to farm laborers, an unsatisfactory tenant or cropsharing system, the boll weevil and the crop failure of 1916" (Adero, 1994:3). However, Carter G. Woodson argued that although these were important factors, economic opportunity was the most important reason for the migration, or blacks would had left earlier (Adero, 1993:3). To say this is to also argue that the importance of economic opportunity and its connection to human freedom suggest the southern black's ideological commitment to the ideas of the Enlightment as actualized in the city. According to Richard Wright, "Negroes, with but minor exceptions, still believe in the hope of economic rewards; they believe in justice, liberty, the integrity of the individual. In the heart of industrial America is a surviving remnant, perchance a saving remnant of passion for freedom, a passion fanned by their national humiliation" (1947:xxv). The surviving remnant Wright is referring to is Chicago.

Both world wars created economic opportunities in the North. As the federal government mobilized American industry for the war effort, blacks were mostly recruited for temporary work, and to their dismay were paid low wages. After both world wars, black migrants faced long periods of unemployment or unsteady work as white soldiers returned from war to reclaim their jobs. In addition, many southern black migrants before and after both world wars were recruited by northern industry to be strikebreakers, to disrupt the efforts of white workers to unionize. Once unionized, white workers used their unions to promote racial segregation on the job; they blocked black workers from entering into the better paying skilled jobs, relegating them to dangerous and unskilled low-paying positions. As southern black migrants overwhelmed northern cities with their numbers, black urban settlements became increasingly larger.

In their classic study, *Black Metropolis* (1962), black anthropologists St. Clair Drake and Horace Cayton argue that since the 1920s, in coexistence with the "Great" migration of blacks from the rural South, residential segregation contributed greatly to the formation of huge black urban settlements or "black ghettos" in Northern industrial cities. The reason being that through restrictive covenants whites geographically constricted black housing patterns, thus encouraging overcrowding and deteriorating housing conditions. Nevertheless, Drake and Cayton make the argument that blacks "[did] not oppose residential segregation with the same vigor that they displayed with attacking [job segregation]" (1962:114). In fact, what blacks demanded was the abolition of restrictive covenants in order that black settlements could expand geographically and "not be confined to the deteriorated slums of the city" (1962:114). In the words of Drake and Cayton, "Negroes want[ed] a normal development in their housing problem—a normal expansion; to be able to move as they need to; to move farther and farther in extension of the area where they live" (1962:113).

What is implied in this is that black civil society—family, neighborhood, school, church, business, voluntary association, and political and civic organization—is buttressed by the territorial maintenance and integrity of black settlements.

According to Drake and Cayton, "Residential segregation is not only supported by the attitudes of white people who object to Negro neighbors—it is also buttressed by the internal structure of the Negro community. Negro politicians and businessmen, preachers and civic leaders, all have a vested interest in maintaining a solid and homogeneous Negro community where their clientele is easily accessible" (1962:115). Referring to Chicago's huge black settlement and its spatial support of black civil society, Drake and Cayton conclude that the "Black Metropolis is an object of pride to Negroes of all strata. It is their city within a city. It is something 'of our own.' It is concrete evidence of one type of freedom—freedom to erect a community in their own image" (1962:115).

This hints at how the social meaning assigned to black settlement space defines the social uses it served for the black community. Accordingly, the shattering of black civil society had as much to do with how the dominant meanings assigned to urban space resulted in spatial forms that corresponded with the "imagined communities" of the white middle class. One way of understanding this is to look at the emergence of an urban rather than a suburban dream within the contemporary urban landscape. In other words, the white middle class has created an urban landscape at the expense of black settlement space, causing social disorder within black civil society, which in turn weakens the ability of blacks to create their own public spaces. These public spaces or "homeplaces," bell hooks argues, are crucial to blacks in creating a culture and politics of resistance:

> The task of making homeplace . . . was about the construction of a safe place where black people could affirm one another and by so doing heal many of the wounds inflicted by racist domination. We could not learn to love or respect ourselves in the culture of white supremacy, on the outside; it was there on the inside, in that "homeplace" that we had the opportunity to grow and develop, to nurture our spirits. (1990:42)

However, the social disorder within black civil society must be placed in the context of how as a social space within the city the black settlement or "black ghetto" has been textually and visually represented as being a "slum" (Goldberg, 1993). Such symbolic representation has undergirded the construction of a binary opposition that defines black settlement space as irrational, ugly, filthy, and immoral and white settlement space as ordered, rational, beautiful, pure, and moral. It is this binary opposition that has provided urban planners with the rationale to remove or dismantle black urban settlements. However, before turning to this issue, I want to look at the wider theoretical question of how social meanings are historically constructed and assigned to particular social spaces within the context of the city. As a way to address this I will review critical approaches to the study of urban space. The following discussion first focuses on the works of Marxist urban political economists, such as David Gordon, David Harvey, and Neil Smith, as well as "culturally sensitive" urban political economists, such as Sharon Zukin. In taking up this issue, I want to offer a criticism of the Marxist urban political economists' view that culture obscures "real" processes of urban redevelopment. Instead, I will argue that culture is a constitutive element in urban redevelopment itself. Furthermore, within this context, I will advance the idea that culture plays an integral role in the production of space, particularly in terms of its textual and visual representations and how such representations are the meaningful basis for constructing "homeplace." This means then that it is in the context of "place making" that blacks form their individual and collective identities as blacks.

Marxists, Urban Political Economy, and the Production of Urban Space

According to the class-struggle perspective of David M. Gordon, the city's spatial organization is the product of conflict between labor and capital. Allegedly, this conflict has produced three historically distinct stages in the spatial formation of the city. The historical specificity of class struggle under each stage of Capitalist accumulation—commercial capital, industrial capital, and monopoly capital—has a unique corresponding city form: the commercial city, the industrial city, and the corporate city. Gordon asserts that just as "capitalist machines" were developed to control workers at the site of production, "capitalist spatial forms" were also developed to maintain capitalist control over the production process (1978:27). The implication is that the different stages of city forms were believed to be "produced by the variety of spatial responses that the capitalist class had to make in order to maintain its social hegemony over the production process" (Gottdiener, 1985:75).

At the turn of the century, the concentration of manufacturing in the industrial city had resulted in the formation of huge working-class settlements near factories located in the central city. One important effect of this was the flight of the middle-class from the central city to the suburbs. According to Gordon, the middle class "no longer worked and lived in the same place; there was now a separation between job and residential location" (1978:44). This meant that the central city was no longer residentially heterogeneous, "instead, the cities had quickly acquired a sharp residential segregation by economic class" (Gordon, 1978:44). Gordon's main argument is that this contributed to the social isolation of the working class. The significance of this is that before factories and working class settlements completely dominated the central-city landscape, the middle class had been supportive of efforts to make industrialists accountable for the deteriorating and unhealthy conditions for which they were responsible in working-class housing districts. With the social and spatial isolation of the working class, the industrialists were more effectively able to repress workers' resistance and enforce labor discipline in the factories.

While the spatial form of the earlier industrial city served to subdue working-class militancy, David Gordon argues that as the working class became more densely concentrated, the industrial city form became more conducive to labor unrest. The reason was that the dense spatial concentration of the industrial working class meant that individual strikes and struggles could more easily spread among neighboring workers (Gordon, 1978:45). In response to heightened labor unrest throughout the late 1880s to the 1890s, individual industrialists suddenly began to move their factories from downtown central-city districts to the suburbs (Gordon, 1978:48-49). Individual industrialists had realized that the dense concentration of workers in a single geographical area within the city encouraged them to frequently compare their work conditions with those of workers in other factories. Industrialists believed this was the cause of the mass wave of unionization and strikes in their factories. The consequence of this move to the suburbs was that working-class housing was no longer packed into dense central zones, but scattered around the metropolitan area and increasingly segmented.

Therefore, the spatial response of the industrialists to strikes in their factories precipitated in part the transition from an industrial to a corporate city form. In addition to the dispersing of industry to the suburbs, the creation and growth of downtown business districts around the 1920s had also contributed to this new city form. As huge corporations had consolidated their monopoly control over their industries and markets they had begun separating their administrative functions from the production process itself and relocating them to downtown business districts. The advantage in relocating their administrative headquarters downtown was that they were near other headquarters, banks, law offices, and advertising agents. "The uneven centralization of headquarters locations," Gordon writes, "quickly surpassed the concentration of industrial employment" (1978:52). He further elaborates that by 1929, "56 percent of the national corporations had located their headquarters in New York or Chicago" (1978:52). For this reason, Gordon concludes that central business districts with their towering skyscrapers embodied in spatial form the centralization of economic power.

While Gordon's analysis focuses on class conflict, David Harvey's focuses on the process of capital accumulation. His work devotes more direct attention to the spatial organization of consumption, its contribution to the process of capital accumulation, and its configuration of urban space, rather than to the labor process. In *The Urban Experience* Harvey asks the question, "How does capital become urbanized, and what are the consequences of that urbanization" (1989:18)? In response, his analysis of urbanization focuses on the circulation of capital through the production and use of the built environment. This reflects his belief that the geographical landscape of capitalism is the expression of flows of capital.

More specifically, Harvey uses the term *flows of capital* to denote the flow of money, labor, and commodities within the geographical space of cities. He argues that what determines a business' investment of capital in building an urban infrastructure is whether or not the spatial arrangement of its built environment is appropriate for the location of particular kinds of economic activity. Put another way, the activities of the industrial and service sectors require a particular kind of built environment to function effectively. The assumption is that the spatial design of cities must facilitate the flow of capital.

Furthermore, the term *built environment* is used by Harvey to indicate that urban landscapes are complex assemblages of various constructions that include roads, buildings, transit systems, and utilities. In other words, what determines the investment of capital in a particular urban landscape is whether its built environment is useful in the process of capital accumulation, particularly in relation to distribution and consumption. In *Social Justice of the City* (1973) Harvey implies that the main function of the built environment of "capitalist" cities is to absorb the surplus that is produced within a Capitalist economy. This means that the decision to invest capital in an urban infrastructure is in part due to whether its built environment facilitates the spatial circulation of goods and services, so as to stimulate demand and consumption.

Harvey develops this further by suggesting that historically, Capitalist cities have been spatially organized around a center. One reason for this stems from the belief that it represents a more efficient way to coordinate the economic activities of capitalism across space. This meant that in the spatial and hierarchical ordering of economic activities, the most key activities were located in the center of cities. For example, in the industrial city, which was organized around mass production, the center of the city was the site for the coordination of raw materials, labor, and equipment. And because the survival of industrial capitalism was based on coordinating mass production with mass consumption, the working class's living spaces, which included housing, schools, churches, stores, and recreation facilities, were located around the center. In other words, the coordination of mass production with mass consumption within the industrial city was achieved through a geographically concentrated built environment and labor force. The idea was that through the centralization of production and the concentration of consumption, the cost and amount of time it took to produce and distribute goods and services over a geographical space was reduced. In effect, this not only contributed to industrial productivity, but it also kept down the price of goods and services, thereby increasing demand and consumption, leading to the realization of business profits.

Because of the spatial organization and technological innovations of industrial production, industrial capitalism's capacity to massively produce went beyond the ability of the industrial city to absorb its surplus, causing business to begin to disinvest in the built environment of the industrial city (Harvey, 1989:34-43). Its inability to absorb surplus caused the commodity markets to become saturated.

This indicated that the geographically concentrated built environment of the industrial city was no longer a viable spatial strategy for the production and circulation of goods and services. In other words, the physical infrastructure and spatial design of the industrial city no longer functioned to increase demand and consumption (Harvey, 1989:28-34). According to Harvey, this is because the buildings that facilitated industrial production and the circulation of goods and services became a hindrance to realizing profits, due to their location. The location occupied by buildings became more valuable than the buildings themselves, therefore, the buildings' use of a location prevented the full realization of that location's value. Harvey suggests that to renew a location's value, the old buildings occupying that location be destroyed and replaced with new buildings. So while a building may be valuable for its functional use, the location it occupies may be of even more value for business, in particular, real estate developers and financial institutions. This assumes that the value of a location not only relates to its exchange or market value, *but also to its potential uses.*

What is highlighted here is the realization of the exchange value benefits of a location through the creation and financing of new use values by real estate developers (Harvey, 1973:165). Further, Harvey believes that the creation of new use values involves shifting the flow of capital away from past investments in the built environment to investments in the building of new urban infrastructures. In doing this, old buildings are devalued and destroyed. The point Harvey is making here is that the survival of capitalism is tied to the continual rebuilding of the built environment of cities:

> Capitalist development has therefore to negotiate a knife-edge path between preserving the exchange values of past capital investments in the built environment and destroying the value of these investments in order to open up fresh room for accumulation. Under capitalism there is, then, a perpetual

struggle in which capital builds a physical landscape appropriate to its own condition at a particular moment in time, only to have to destroy it, usually in the course of a crisis, at a subsequent point in time. The temporal and geographic ebb and flow of investment in the built environment can be understood only in terms of such a process. The effects of the internal contradictions of capitalism, when projected into the specific context of fixed and immobile investment in the built environment, are thus writ large in the historical geography of the landscape. (1973:125)

Another way of understanding this is by exploring how the failure of the industrial city's built environment to absorb surplus led to a crisis in consumption, referred to as "underconsumption." According to Harvey, the solution to this crisis was to destroy the spatially concentrated built environment of the industrial city, to replace it with a more spatially dispersed urban landscape. Through geographical expansion, the housing construction and real estate industries had more land and space available to create new use values. What Harvey asserts is that a spatially deconcentrated built environment provides capitalism with more opportunities to invest in transforming and expanding the urban infrastructure.

One major example he points to is the "urban sprawl" which began dominating urban landscapes around the 1950s and 1960s. Also known as "suburbanization," this geographical expansion of the urban infrastructure was debt financed by the state, leading Harvey to call the "urban sprawl" the "Keynesian city" (Harvey, 1989:37:39). As a way to encourage the real estate and housing construction industries and financial institutions to invest in the geographical expansion of the urban infrastructure, the Keynesian policies of the state contributed to the creation of sprawling, extensive, single-family housing developments, mainly through credit financing. Not only did this stimulate the building, real estate, and banking industries, it also reinforced the energy, auto, and highway construction industries. Harvey argues that the reason why state-managed debt financing was somewhat effective in overcoming underconsumption was because it was linked to the geographical dispersion of the urban landscape. He says that

> debt-financed infrastructure formation was accompanied by strong processes of spatial reorganization of the urban system. Long reduced to a commodity, . . . land speculation had also been a potent force making for urban sprawl and rapid transitions in spatial organization, particularly in the United States. . . . But it took the rising economic power of individuals to appropriate space for their own exclusive purposes through debt-financed homeownership and debt-financed access to transport services (auto purchases as well as highway), to create the "suburban solution" to the underconsumption problem . . . suburbanization . . . marked post-war urbanization to an extraordinary degree. It meant the mobilization of effective demand through the total restructuring of space so as to make the consumption of products of the auto, oil, rubber, and construction industries a necessity rather than a luxury . . . after 1945, suburbanization was part of a package of moves to insulate capitalism against the threat of crises of underconsumption. (1989:39)

The flow of capital investment into the formation of suburbs Harvey argues, also contributed to the abandonment and destruction of neighborhoods in the central city. When the mostly white unionized blue-collar workers left for the suburbs, so did their manufacturing jobs, leaving factory buildings and equipment to idle and devalue. Real estate developers, city governments, and financial institutions destroyed the devalued factory buildings and equipment in order to make the locations they occupied more profitable. Through Keynesian demand-side urbanization, real estate developers and banks were encouraged by federal policies to channel investments toward rebuilding the location of the old manufacturing district into a central business district (Harvey, 1989:40-42). Harvey argues that one result of dismantling the old manufacturing district to make centralized locations for the headquarters of corporations is devaluing of the adjacent housing stock of old working-class neighborhoods.

One explanation for this is that in changing the particular utility of a central location—because the centrality of that location determines the usefulness of other locations nearby—disinvestment will occur in the housing stock of those neighborhoods immediately surrounding the central business district. Harvey believes that this process continues to cause a devaluation in the physical infrastructure of those neighborhoods, eventually making them prime targets for land speculation and real estate development.

Much of the redevelopment of neighborhoods adjacent to the central business district was not intended to expand or improve the housing stock for poor and working-class black people living in the central city. In fact, most urban development was directed toward expanding the built environment of the central business district. A consequence of this is that it reduced the availability of inner-city housing for blacks, causing them to live in very overcrowded housing conditions. In sum, the land-use practices of city planners, real estate developers, and financiers contributed to the creation of overcrowded and deteriorated housing conditions, inflated rents, landlord neglect, abandonment of buildings, and the curtailment of municipal services. Harvey argues that this, paired with the relocation of high-paying unionized factory jobs to the suburbs, was responsible for the formation of inner-city black ghettos.

One major problem with Harvey's view of the formation of the black ghetto is that he sees it as simply being a logical consequence of the spatialization of capitalism. This is similar to Gordon's view, except that Gordon sees the spatial formation of capitalism as being the result of class struggle, a class struggle that originates from the logic of the production process itself. For Gordon, the dispersion of the white working class and industry from the central city to the suburbs was capitalism's attempt to exert control over the labor process through the organization of urban space. The consequence of capitalism's spatial reordering of the city is the creation of conditions that gave rise to inner-city black ghettos: "Surrounding the central business district were emptying manufacturing areas, depressed from the desertion of large plants, barely surviving on the light and competitive industries left behind. Next to those districts were the old working-class districts, often transformed into 'ghettos' locked into the cycle of central city manufacturing decline" (Gordon, 1978:54).

But unlike Gordon's argument that the spatial organization of the city is mainly to facilitate Capitalist production, Harvey also includes Capitalist consumption. Nevertheless, both authors' interpretations of the production of urban space are informed by the functional logic of reproduction.

The Problem of Reproduction in Marxian Urban Political Economy

Both Gordon's and Harvey's arguments reduce the "built environment" of the city to a function of Capitalist accumulation and expansion. For example, as political-economic Marxists, Gordon and Harvey both believe that "the processes of capitalist development are materialized in space, almost through a one-to-one correspondence with the actual forms of the built environment" (Gottdiener, 1985:121). What this means is that the spatial forms of the built environment are "appearances and empirically observed regularities that are epiphenomenal reflections of underlying and largely invisible social relations" (Gottdiener, 1985:158). Gottdiener argues that "the task facing marxists has always been both to identify the deeper social forces affecting surface events and to show how their laws of motion percolate, so to speak, through levels of social organization to determine empirically observed regularities" (1985:158).

This suggests that a realist epistemology informs the Marxian political economic interpretation of urban space. However, its realism has tended to move towards a positivistic, causal logic to explain the relationship of urban space to Capitalist development. The result of this move is that theoretical explanations become equated with prediction. Put another way, Marxists assume that they can predict changes in the spatial form of cities by deterministically linking them to the logic of Capitalist development (Gottdiener, 1985:159). This is because positivistic discourse has led some Marxists to believe that by directly observing the spatial form of cities they can verify empirically the political-economic logic of capitalism. And that through this verification, they can predict the actual correspondence of a spatial form to a specific stage in Capitalist development. In general, what a positivist discourse assumes is "that theoretical evidence corresponds to an objectively verifiable reality and the task of the theorist is to unmask such a correspondence" (Giroux, 1992b:6). Or, as Aronowitz states: "The positivist expects that anything that can be theorized is based on corresponding 'sense-data'" (1990:241).

The turn toward a positivistic discourse within Marxian political economy succumbs to the use of the logic of reproduction to explain urban space. From the perspective of reproduction theory, the underlying logic of capital is its inherent tendency to subsume urban space under its domination. This reduces the autonomy of urban forms to "moments" of capital. What is being suggested is that Marxian political economy reduces urban space to an object of the means of production. For Marxists, the material objects that constitute the means of production are those that are processed by labor, such as raw materials, and the tools that are used in production (Gottdiener, 1985:124). Gottdiener elaborates that in the means of production "other objects, although not tools themselves, facilitate the use of tools, like buildings, stores, harbors, roads, and land, are also included in this group" (1985:124). With David Harvey in mind, Gottdiener concludes: "Thus the built environment, as political economists define it, is part of the means of production, specifically the means of labor. The reduction of space merely to this aspect results in certain important limitations in the ability of neo-Marxists to explain aspects of spatial production" (1988:124). What I have in mind is the inability of neo-Marxists to explain the relationship of the cultural politics of race to spatial production in the city, which will be discussed later.

By defining the built environment as part of the means of production, urban space is reduced to an instrumental function of capital accumulation and expansion. It is important to remind ourselves that the reason for this functionalism within Marxian political economy has to do with its uncritical appropriation of positivist ideology:

> For instance, in orthodox Marxist theories of culture and art, the notions of multiple causality and indeterminacy are replaced by cause and effect models informed by theories of scientific explanation based on the instrumental logic of lawfulness, falsifiability, quantification, and formulaic simplicity. The instrumentalism and technical rationality that underlie Marxist theory also finds expression in those theories of the state in which the latter is accorded no relative autonomy and as such is reduced to a purely instrumental role. (Aronowitz and Giroux, 1991:127)

Marxist discussions of the political economy of urban space have contained these same tendencies. In particular, the instrumental and technical logic that informs functionalist Marxist theories about urban space suggests that space has intrinsic uses. Such a view, Rosalyn Deutsche writes, "makes it seem that individual locations within the city and the spatial organization of the city as a whole contain an inherent meaning determined by the imperative to fulfill needs that are presupposed to be natural, simply practical"

(1991a:159). Therefore, because the spatial order is seen through the lens of function it appears to be controlled by natural, mechanical, or organic laws. This leads to space being fetishized as a physical entity severed from its social production, making the city appear as though it speaks for itself. According to Deutsche, "The organization and shaping of the city as well as the attribution of meanings to space are social processes. Spatial forms are social structures" (1991:160). In naming them "social structures," she refers to the recognition that the production and uses of the city are conflictual processes. She summarizes:

> Represented as an independent object, [space] appears to exercise control over the very people who produce and use it. The impression of objectivity is real to the extent that the city is alienated from the social life of its inhabitants. The functionalization of the city, which presents space as neutral, merely utilitarian, is, then filled with politics. For the notion that the city speaks for itself conceals the identity of those who speak through the city. (1991a:160)

Space as Location or Space as Place?

J. Nicholas Entrikin in *The Betweenness of Place* (1991) argues that the representation of space as objective and neutral trivializes the particularity of place, that is, "place becomes either location or a set of generic relations" (1991:5). Representations of space as objective have much to do with how the discourse of science has reduced space to a rational mathematical concept. Or, as Henri Lefebvre states: "The science of space . . . can be viewed as a science of formal space, that is to say, close to mathematics; a science which employs such concepts as construction density, network analysis, critical path analysis and program evaluation and review techniques" (1977:342). In addition to this, Harvey argues that space must be understood in relation to time, perceived also as a rational mathematical concept. This way of defining space and time is deeply implicated in the material processes of social reproduction. Because of this, Harvey claims that space and time are both social and objective (1990a:422). By this he means that as social constructs, space and time get defined by the material processes of social reproduction. As Harvey states: "The objective definitions must in the first instance be understood, not by appeal to the world of thoughts and ideas, but from the study of material processes of social reproduction" (1990a:422).

This move allows Harvey to situate his seemingly objective definition of space and time within what he calls a materialist perspective on the historical geography of space and time (1990a:422). He introduces this perspective by arguing that the "fetishism of commodities" is closely related to "the geography of commodity production and the definitions of space and time embedded in the practices of commodity production and capital circulation" (1990:423). Put another way, the exploitive and oppressive conditions that wage laborers have to endure, when producing the goods we consume daily, appear to us as invisible:

> We cannot tell from looking at a commodity whether it has been produced by happy laborers working in a cooperative in Italy, grossly exploited laborers working under conditions of apartheid in South Africa, or wage laborers protected by adequate labor legislation and wage agreements in Sweden. The grapes that sit upon the supermarket shelves are mute; we cannot see the fingerprints of exploitation upon them or tell immediately what part of the world they are from. (Harvey, 1990:422)

Harvey therefore proposes that "to penetrate the veil of fetishism and discover what lies behind it" (1990:423), we have to know how space and time get defined by the systems of commodity production and exchange. With this in mind, he asserts that the rational mathematical definitions

of space and time, as well as the spatial and temporal practices that follow, are intrinsic to the political-economic logic
of Western capitalism. As Harvey explains, the "elimina-
tion of spatial barriers and the struggle to 'annihilate space
through time' is essential to the whole dynamic of capital
accumulation" (1990:425). Accordingly, because the price
of labor time is fundamental to the making of money, the
concern for efficiency in production, exchange, commerce,
and administration is what Harvey claims determines the
Capitalist's logic of decision (1989:179).

It is the concern for efficiency that has lead Western
capitalism to embrace a definition of time as something
that could be measured and represented with respect to
clearly defined rational mathematical principles. According
to Harvey, this contributed to technologically revolutioniz-
ing communication and transportation and to rapidly speed-
ing up the movement of goods, people, information, and
messages, thereby contributing immensely to capitalism's
geographic mobility. For one thing, when employed as a
threat, geographic mobility gave companies an advantage
in bargaining sessions with unions. This permitted
Capitalists through subcontracting arrangements and home-
work to create much more "flexible" labor markets, causing
a rapid growth in part-time and temporary work. Harvey
argues that labor market flexibility allowed Capitalists to
quickly reallocate labor power "from one sector of production to another to meet seasonal or other fluctuations in
demand" (1991:71).

In addition, Harvey claims that the deployment of new
technological innovations and organizational techniques in
the labor process reduced the turnover time in production.
The reasons for this had much to do with the desire of
Capitalists wanting to create greater flexibility in the labor
process. That is, new technologies (robots, automation) and
new organizational forms ("just-in-time" inventory-flow
delivery systems) in production were deployed to speed up
and cut down radically on stocks required to keep the production flow going. "But the speed-up in production entails

parallel speed-up in exchange (marketing and banking) and consumption" (1991:76). According to Harvey, in the realm of cultural production, technological innovations in telecommunications accelerated the turnover time in consumption habits and lifestyle. This is because "the lifetime of consumption images, as opposed to more tangible objects like autos and refrigerators, is almost instantaneous" (1990:427). Finally, as for the turnover time in exchange, new computerized information systems provide instant data analysis, giving companies the "capacity for instantaneous response to changes in exchange rates, fashions and tastes, and moves by competitors" (1989:159).

Because of capitalism's new technological innovations, the acceleration of turnover times along with the shortening of the time horizon for decision making has resulted in the "annihilation of space through time." As Harvey states: "The breaking down and reorganization of spatial barriers has been one of the chief means whereby capitalism has sustained itself in the 20th century" (1991:76). What Harvey is getting at is that time in accordance with the political-economic logic of capital accumulation and expansion has been coupled with new spatial configurations in production, exchange, and consumption. He concludes that the acceleration of turnover time in production, exchange and consumption has provided Capitalists with the capacity to geographically disperse the built environment of cities (i.e., the urban sprawl or suburbanization) so as to facilitate the absorption of surplus. In the words of Harvey:

> Capitalism, Marx insists, necessarily accelerates spatial integration within the world market, the conquest and liberation of space, and the annihilation of space by time. In so doing it accentuates rather than undermines the significance of space. Capitalism has survived, says Lefebvre "only by occupying space, by producing space." The ability to find a 'spatial fix' to its inner contradictions has proven one of its saving graces . . . the community of capital requires

the geographical deepening and widening of processes of capital accumulation at an accelerating
rate. (1989:190)

According to Harvey, the annihilation of space by time
to facilitate the rapid flow of capital—of money, labor, and
commodities—over space, has meant continuously destroying and replacing the built landscapes of cities with new
ones. In other words, capitalism's quest to accelerate
turnover time has been matched with a general process of
continuous reshaping of geographical landscapes, involving
processes as diverse as suburbanization, deindustrialization
and restructuring, gentrification, and urban renewal (Harvey,
1989:192). The term used by Harvey to denote this process
is *creative destruction*. However, implicit in this term is
an assumption that the constant reshaping of urban landscapes has made land into a purely financial asset, a form of
"fictitious capital" (Harvey, 1989:191). This means then
that landownership amounts to a property right over some
form of future revenue. Landowners therefore play an active
role in coordinating the flow of capital onto and through
the land to enhance future rents:

> By perpetually striving to put the land under its "high-
> est and best use," they create a sorting device that
> shifts land uses and forces allocations of capital and
> labor that might not otherwise occur. They also inject
> a fluidity and dynamism into the use of land which
> would otherwise be hard to generate and so adjust the
> use of land to social requirements. They thereby shape
> the geographical structure of production, exchange,
> and consumption, the technical and social division of
> labor in space, and the socioeconomic spaces of repro-
> duction, and invariably exert a powerful influence
> over investment in physical infrastructure. They typ-
> ically compete for that particular pattern of develop-
> ment, that particular bundle of investments and activ-
> ities, which has the best prospects for enhancing
> future rents. (Harvey, 1989:96-97)

By rendering landownership subservient to money power, space appears as homogeneous. The reason for this, Harvey argues, has to do with how land markets totally pulverize and fragment space into freely alienable parcels of private property, to be bought and traded at will upon the market. Or, in Harvey's words, "It took something more to consolidate the actual use of space as universal, homogeneous, objective, and abstract in social practice . . . [t]he 'something more' that came to dominate was private property in land and the buying and selling of space as commodity" (1989:177). It is in being rendered a commodity that space, according to Marxists, is believed to consist of interchangeable fragments. In other words, "exchangeability implies interchangeabilty" (Lefebvre, 1979:3) These fragments are interchangeable by virtue that they are qualitatively comparable for purposes of exchange. By qualitatively comparing the multiple locations that fragment space, space is treated as something that is objective. And to view space as objective is to assume that it is divorced from how we as socially constituted subjects with particular racial, sexual, gendered, and class identities give space-specific cultural meanings.

This perception of space as objective and devoid of any particular cultural meaning has influenced J. Nicholas Entrikin (1991) to distinguish between "space as location" and "space as place." With regard to the latter, place is understood as the context of human actions. Entrikin implies this when he says that "the significance of place is associated with the fact that as actors we are always situated in place and that the context of our actions contribute to our sense of identity" (1991:4). He concludes that "the significance of place in modern life is associated with this fact of "situatedness" and the closely related issues of identity and action" (1991:3).

What is important about all of this is that place and identity are bonded together, and culture is the glue that bonds them. That is, "[a]s agents in the world we are always 'in place,' much as we are always 'in culture.' For this reason our relations to place and culture become elements in the construction of our individual and collective identities" (Entrikin, 1991:1). Or, as Roger Friedland notes, "Place is the fusion of space and experience, a space filled with meaning, a source of identity" (1992:14). But we give meaning to specific places in relation to our actions as individuals and as members of groups. "Places are significant" Entrikin observes, "not because of their inherent value, but rather because we assign values to them in relation to our projects" (1991:16).

Yet, whenever space is rendered universal, homogeneous, objective, and abstract, place is stripped of its meaning and reduced to location. In other words, "the only meaning of place [becomes] that of the location of one object in relation to others" (Entrikin, 1990:10). Critical of this view, Henri Lefebvre argues that through the notion of a science of space, "urban space, which was formerly discussed in connection with community culture, was isolated from the context; it appeared as a given, as a specific dimension of spatial organization" (1977:340). He goes on to say that in modern urban planning theory "space was [perceived as] objective and 'pure'; it was a scientific object and hence had a neutral character" (1977:340). "Modern urban development," Kenneth Frampton writes, "has favoured the proliferation of a universal, privatized, placeless domain" (1988:340). Frampton concludes that "it was this same phenomenon which led planner[s] to coin such terms as 'community without propinquity' or 'non-place urban realm' as slogans with which to rationalize the total loss of the civic domain" (1988:58). Again, this is related to the defining of place as a location in space.

The Marxists' perspective of the political economy of urban space has strongly contributed to the reinforcement of the perception of place as simply the location of objects and events in space. That is, "places are translated into homogeneous spaces, and events and objects are conceptually distinguished from their locations" (Entrikin, 1991:43). In particular, the Marxists' concept of "uneven development" perpetuates the view of place as the location of objects and events in space. Such a concept implies the assumption that the very logic of the process of Capitalist expansion necessitates that the search for profits leads to the investment of capital in some areas and disinvestment in others (Entrikin, 1991:48). In support of this, Harvey writes,

> Factories and fields, schools, churches, shopping centres and parks, roads and railways litter a landscape that has been indelibly and irreversibly carved out according to the dictates of capitalism. Again, this physical transformation has not progressed evenly. Vast concentrations of productive power here contrast with relatively empty regions there. Tight concentrations of activity in one place contrast with sprawling far-flung development in another. All of this adds up to what we call "uneven geographical development" of capitalism. (1982:373)

In a similar vein, the idea of uneven development is the premise of Neil Smith's theory of urban restructuring and gentrification. He argues that through sustained disinvestment by landlords and financial institutions, the built environment of central-city locations or neighborhoods is intentionally left to deteriorate. The purpose behind disinvestment is that it will lower land values and in the future encourage more lucrative reinvestment (1986:238-52). So for those Marxists interested in the political economy of urban space, "places are differentiated in terms of capital investment" (Entrikin, 1991:47). This has lead to the perception that as locations places are like "re-usable containers" ready to be "emptied" or "filled" with objects. For example:

> The power to create versatile architectural forms, and minutely to subdivide, organize, and reorganize every aspect within, made the built environment both a conceptually and actually emptiable and re-useable space or container. Seeing and using space

as a container at the architectural level merges with
the awareness of geographical space as a surface or
volume in which events occur. . . . It means that
events and space are conceptually separable and that
one is only contingently related to the other. People,
things and processes are not anchored to a place—are
not essentially and necessarily of a place. (Sack,
1986:90)

What is being argued here is that when defined as a
location, place is viewed as something separate, something
external. Rosalyn Deutsche argues that when "[r]epre-
sented as an independent object, [space] appears to exercise
control over the very people who produce and use it"
(1991:160). Thus, the people and things that are supposedly "contained" in a place are thought of as objects to be
manipulated within the built environment of cities. This
view, place as the location of objects in space, is very
accepting of instrumental rationality. That is, people and
things are given importance only in terms of their function
with respect to locations. Such a perception favors those
groups whose interests dominate decisions about the organization of space. The reason is that "the exigencies of
human social life provide a single meaning that necessitates proper uses of the city—proper places for its residents" (Deutsche, 1991a:160). Accordingly, Deutsche
writes, "The prevailing goals of the existing spatial structure are regarded as, by definition, beneficial to all"
(1991a:160).
     Through the use of the concept of "uneven develop-
ment" political-economic Marxists have argued that in fact
the existing spatial structure has not been "beneficial to
all." Because as Neil Smith has pointed out, disinvestment
in central-city neighborhoods also entails a strategy of even-
tual reinvestment by real estate developers and bankers,
leading to middle-class gentrification and the eviction of
poor and working-class communities. Most political-economic Marxists would simply see this as a conflict between

labor and capital, a conflict over whose interests will dominate the organization of space. Urban struggles which therefore attempt to reclaim gentrifying neighborhoods around specific definitions of place and identity are rooted in "false consciousness."

In other words, the holding on to a specific place as a source of identity is believed to be an "ideological" response to the weakening of spatial barriers; that is, to the ability of Capitalists because of new technological innovations to "annihilate space through time." Referring to this, Harvey asserts, "Such a quest for visible and tangible marks of identity is readily understandable in the midst of fierce time-space compression" (1991:427). However, he indirectly associates this quest for place identity with false consciousness, because he does not believe places are differentiated by cultural identities. Instead, the differentiation between places is the outcome of different levels of capital investment, as in the case of uneven development. When social critics believe that culture is the basis for the formation of place, "geographical differentiations," Harvey writes, "appear to be historical residuals rather than actively reconstituted features within the capitalist mode of production" (1991:416). From this perspective, the role that culture plays in the formation of place is secondary:

> In the [orthodox Marxist] arguments concerning areal differentiation, places are differentiated in terms of capitalist investment and functional specialization. Local or regional consciousness, or more generally, culture, is seen as derivative of the functional specialization created by the economy. Such consciousness is viewed either as an historical artifact left over from an earlier age or as a response to a more fundamental, utilitarian logic. Difference is created, but specificity is lost. . . . The implication is that culture is epiphenomenal, lagging behind and being pulled by these more fundamental forces. (Entrikin, 1991:47)

The Cultural Politics of
Revelopment and Gentrification

Such a perception allows for the neo-Marxists' assumption that culture obscures "ideologically" how the Capitalist economy of space is responsible for the formation of place. From this point of view, it can be argued that gentrification results from the uneven development in metropolitan land markets. But this is believed to be obscured because the urban design and architectural forms of gentrified neighborhoods are culturally coded to visually represent an identity of place. This is done, however, by using urban and architectural forms that preserve and echo the past. What is being argued by some Marxists is that through cultural production, urban designers and architects, in collaboration with developers, are able to stimulate middle-class consumption in the urban real estate market, by either recreating or recuperating past urban and architectural forms. "The new middle class," Michael Jager adds, "does not buy simply a deteriorated house when it takes over a slum, nor does it just buy into future 'equity,' it just buys into the past" (1986:81).

In recreating the past in urban form urban designers and architects have been responsible for the creation of status distinctions, by establishing a new criteria of taste in art as well as in urban living. To restate, this cultivation of the aesthetic faculty is associated with the attempt to appropriate history. However, this has not only been done to encourage conspicuous consumption, but also to signify social distinction through the consumption and reproduction of past history. Jean Baudrillard argues that the predilection of the new middle class for antiques is an example of how it attempts to socially distinguish itself. He writes, "The taste for the bygone is characterized by the desire to transcend the dimension of economic success, to consecrate a social success or a privileged position in a redundant, culturalized, symbolic sign. The bygone is, among other things, social success that seeks a legitimacy,

heredity, a noble sanction" (1981:43). Neal Smith elaborates on this by suggesting that "the pursuit of difference,
diversity, and distinction forms the basis for the new urban
ideology" (1987:168), and that this pursuit "embodies a
search for diversity as long as it is highly ordered, and a
glorification of the past as long as it is safely brought into
the present" (1987:168).

Nevertheless, neo-Marxists are quick to point out that
this urban ideology, and its production of "taste cultures"
and therefore social distinctions, is not the cause for uneven
development and gentrification. Instead, the argument is
that taste and culture are deliberately deployed by urban
designers and architects to conceal the "real basis of economic distinctions" (Harvey, 1991:78). Or in Harvey's
words: "Since the most successful ideological effects are
those which have no words, and ask no more than complicitous silence, the production of symbolic capital serves ideological functions because the mechanisms through which
it contributes to the reproduction of the established order
and the perpetuation of domination remain hidden"
(1991:78). What is believed "hidden" is that gentrification is
rooted in the structural dynamics of advanced capitalism.
That is, "the inevitable falling rate of profit and the over-
production of commodities have led to a crisis of capitalism" (Jager, 1986:38), which can only to be resolved by shifting capital investment from the sphere of production to the
built environment (Harvey, 1989; Smith, 1986). Neil Smith
and David Harvey maintain that the reason for this shift in
the built environment is that "the most profitable opportunities for capital accumulation are those devalorized neighborhoods where capitalized ground rent is significantly
below potential ground rent" (Beauregard, 1986:39).
Gentrification, in other words, operates mostly to counter-
act the falling rate of profit. Culture here is not seen as
being constitutive of place. As in the case of gentrification,
culture is perceived in terms of its "ideological function,"
which is to conceal the "fundamental forces" that are essential to the formation of place.

In *Landscapes of Power* Sharon Zukin argues that "gentrification appeared as a rediscovery, an attempt to recapture the value of place" (1991:192). Implicit in Zukin's remark is the idea that place, and therefore gentrification, is a cultural formation. For example, she goes on to say that the process of gentrification constructs social space or habitus on the basis of cultural rather than economic capital (1991:192). Elsewhere, she adds that "[g]entrifiers viewed the dilapidated built environment of the urban vernacular from . . . the perspective of aesthetics and history. Nevertheless, she concludes that "their demand to preserve old buildings—with regard to cultural rather than economic value—helped constitute a market for the special characteristics of place" (1991:192). What this means is that the process of gentrification is not only mediated by the market but also by the cultural values and claims of potential gentrifiers. This means that working-class residents exert a weaker claim to the downtown than the cultural values of gentrifiers. It is therefore the "gentifiers' capacity for attaching themselves to history [that] gives them license to "reclaim" the downtown for their own use" (Zukin, 1991:193). Zukin writes:

> Gentrification joins economic claim to space with a cultural claim that gives priority to the demands of historic preservationists and art producers. In this view, "historic" buildings can only be appreciated to their maximum value if they are explained, analyzed, and understood as part of an aesthetic discourse, such as the history of architecture and art. Such buildings rightfully belong to people who have the resources to search for the original building plans and study their house in the context of the architect's career. They belong to residents who restore mahogany paneling and buy copies of nineteenth-century faucets instead of those who prefer aluminum siding. (1991:193)

What Zukin is clarifying is that gentrification began as a cultural movement to recover the past architectural history of cities. She therefore describes the original gentrifiers as historic preservationists and artists who were also referred to as "urban pioneers." They became pervasive because their cultural preferences were incorporated into the official norms of neighborhood renewal and city planning (1991:192). City planners used the cultural preferences of the original gentrifiers to attract the new middle class to buy and restore houses in certain "historic" downtown areas. This was done by declaring those areas as historical landmarks, consequently restricting other land-use patterns downtown. Nonetheless, it was real estate developers and large property owners that eventually became the dominant force behind incorporating the cultural values of gentrifiers into downtown commercial land markets.

Sharon Zukin goes on to argue that the cultural values of a specific place—those areas downtown declared as historical landmarks—served as a springboard for the "commercial revitalization" of downtown. The result is that the aesthetic appeal of gentrification has been abstracted into objects of cultural consumption, hence the rise downtown in art galleries, gourmet restaurants, museums, speciality shops, and nightclubs, all of which attempt to replicate some "authentic" characteristic of a city's past cultural history. Also, "commercial revitalization" has given a boost to tourism through the transformation of architectural designs of past urban landscapes into objects of visual consumption through reconstruction and rehabilitation (Zukin, 1991:206). As a result, the past forms of urban landscapes are "decontextualized" to create an "authentic" sense of place (Zukin, 1991:195). Thus, by turning downtown into a "landscape of consumption," the market has opened public spaces to private consumption. That is, "the cultural values of place [are] finally abstracted into market culture" (Zukin, 1991:195). The consequence of this, Zukin says, is that "gentrification is transformed from a place-defining into a market-defining process" (1991:215).

Implicit in Zukin's comment is the presumption that the cultural value of place and the market is not mutually

constitutive. Instead, Zukin believes that culture is inde-
pendently produced but has been incorporated into the consumer market, leading her to conclude that "cultural consumption has had a positive effect on capital accumulation
in real estate development" (1991:260). In other words, culture is viewed simply as a function of capital investment.
For example, according to Zukin, as "cultural strategies of
visual consumption," gentrification and the "new" tourism
must be understood in terms of how they are articulated
with the service economy (1991:259). She goes on to say
that "[a]lthough [gentrification and the new tourism] manip-
ulate and capitalize on symbols—hence their association
with "symbolic capital"—they produce real economic
value" (1991:59). With this in mind, Zukin concludes that

> to analyze cultural capital in only symbolic terms
> misses its relevance to structural transformation.
> For this reason I have turned around Frederic
> Jameson's assertion that "architecture is the symbol
> of capitalism" and suggested that in an advance ser-
> vice economy, architecture is the capital of symbol-
> ism. . . . Cultural goods and services truly constitute
> real capital—so long as they are integrated as com-
> modities in the market-based circulation of capital.
> (1991:260)

What is being suggested is that when commodified and
made into objects of visual consumption, the aesthetics and
culture of an architectural form are "decontextualized" or
severed from the past history of place. Within this context,
architectural forms act to signify an "imaginative" place
which, Zukin argues, becomes the basis for turning public
spaces (e.g., the street) into private spaces of consumption.
Or in Zukin's words, "a gentrified neighborhood is not so
much a literal place as a cultural oscillation between the
prosaic reality of the contemporary inner city and an imaginative reconstruction of the area's past" (1991:194).

Nonetheless, I would strongly suggest that the imaginative reconstruction of an area's past has just as much to

do with the formation of identity. What I am responding to in Zukin's work is how she reduces the production of urban culture to a function of capital accumulation in real estate development. Within this perspective urban designs and architectural forms are only seen in terms of the visual spaces of consumption they produce for real estate capital (Zukin, 1991:260). Culture is therefore seen in terms of how it "directly mediates economic power by both conforming to and structuring norms of market-driven investment, production, and consumption" (Zukin, 1991:39). By using the word *conforming,* Zukin privileges the economic, which is captured in the following passage:

> Without neglecting the enormous part played by architecture and urban form in the symbolic attachment of place, we must emphasize how much they are influenced by markets. What buildings and districts look like, who uses them, their diversity or homogeneity, how long they last before being torn down: these qualities reflect the spatial and temporal constraints of a market culture. (1991:40)

Again, by "market culture" Zukin is implying the mediating role of culture in "market-driven investment, production and consumption" (1991:39). What she is getting at is how through urban and architectural design, landscapes of production (i.e., the built environment of the old industrial city) become objects of visual consumption. She goes on to argue that this "prepared the way for a shift of economic perspective" (1991:256). She concludes that "the image of industry grew more visual than visceral, more immediately perceived than historically embedded" (1991:257).

The problem with Sharon Zukin's analysis is that the "visual" is equated with seeing as a process of perceiving the real world rather than pleasure in looking. By interpreting seeing as the pleasure derived from looking, the argument can be made that as signifiers racial and ethnic difference plays a significant role in constructing how we visually consume urban space. Rosalyn Deutsche in support notes that "[t]he image and act of looking are understood to be relations highly mediated by fantasies that structure and are structured by difference" (1991a:132). This means that the visual consumption of space "is, in the first instance, a set of social relations" (Deutsche, 1991a:132). In contrast to Sharon Zukin, David Harvey, and Neil Smith, Deutsche concludes that because of this "visual space can never be innocent or assumed to reflect, either directly or through contrived mediations, 'real' social relations that reside in the economic relations producing the built environment" (1991:132). The political economy of urban space therefore intersects and is complicated by visual space.

Furthermore, when manufacturing visual space in the built environment, capital investments are bound up with images and fantasies about racial difference, thereby linking the politics of race and ethnicity to the process of place making. What this means is that place must be understood at once as the relative location of objects in the world, and as the meaningful context of human action. As Yi-Fu Tuan states, "Place is not only a fact to be explained in the broader frame of space, but it is also a reality to be clarified and understood from the perspectives of the people who have given it meaning" (cited in Entrikin, 1991:10).

In this sense, the restoration of the past architectural history of cities suggests that urban designers, urban planners, and architects assign meaning to place by linking the pleasure of looking to a nostalgia for a "traditional city." However, implicit in this nostalgia for the past is a utopianism that appeals to neoconservative values such as nation, authority, tradition, and loyalty, except that this is in relation to the present (Levitas, 1990:187). More specifically, Ruth Levitas argues that within the neoconservative utopia, the past is translated in such a way that "the definition and representation of 'heritage' is used to delineate 'us,' the members of the nation, in a way which reinforces old hierarchies and excludes and subordinates some citizens, particularly in terms of race" (1990:188). Therefore, the utopian project of urban planners, designers and architects has much to do with "the continuation of the myth of the all white city" (Keil, 1990:113).

The "continuation of this myth" is related to whether the nostalgic appeal for the "traditional city" is an expression of white fear of the Other. In *Dreaming the Rational City* (1986), M. Christine Boyer points out that in general, early twentieth-century city planners were fearful of the "urban masses." The reason for this fear stems from the middle-class belief that the physical environment of the city was an unnatural and unhealthy location for human beings. This attitude was premised on the idea that the physical decay of the urban environment, due to overcrowding and congestion, was the cause for the city's disorder and inharmoniousness. Somehow this was seen as being responsible for the moral and behavioral decay of the "urban masses," which led to social unrest and political disorder in the city (1986:16). For example, Boyer notes that "[t]he fear of riots and street conflict was constant. The untrained, unorganized poor masses in the city center appeared to the [planners] to be a submerged and undisciplined class beneath the range of cooperation; they seemed suspicious and contemptuous of all constituted authority" (1986:16). Having made this point, she goes on to argue that city planning was centered around disciplining and regulating the lives of the urban masses. Boyer concludes with the argument that city planners operated under the basic premise "that the physical environment itself could discipline humans to achieve a harmonious order with their urban world" (1986:14).

Through the development of park and boulevard systems, early city planners believed that they could establish harmony and order within the congested city by creating natural green spaces. Their implied assumption was that "nature" would have a civilizing influence on the urban masses. According to Boyer, "the devastations and degradations of congested city environments were displaced through images of a rural order infused across the fabric of the city" (1986:37). Elaborating further she argues that "the fears of social unrest [were believed to be] dispelled by the

calming presence of open vistas and pastoral promenades"
(1986:37). This "back to nature movement" was also complimented by the neoclassical architectural movement.

It was accepted at the time that the aesthetic forms of
neoclassical architecture appealed to civic order and virtues
by grouping all public buildings around a civic plaza. Also,
emanating from the civic plaza were streets that "offer a
variety of vistas in every direction, broken here and there by
plazas, fountains, and statuary" (Boyer, 1986:44). The inten-
tion of early city planners was to link such civic ideas as
patriotism to stylized ceremonial spaces. In addition, the
reason why neoclassical architectural design was seen as
an embodiment of civic virtues was because its aesthetics
were believed to reflect the qualities of order, proportion,
rhythm, equilibrium, purity, and harmony. "The city
became a backdrop for reality; it posited eternal order and
civic meaning in place of physical disorder, personal void,
and political and economic exploitation" (Boyer, 1986:50).
Interestingly, Boyer mentions how the quality of purity was
associated with whiteness, and whiteness with cleanliness
and orderliness (1986:44). In fact, Chicago was the proto-
type of the "Great White City" during the World
Columbian Exposition in 1893. And as Boyer notes, "The
Great White City symboliz[ed] purity and light, it stood as
the climatic expression of a more trustful national unity"
(1986:46). The visual space of the "traditional city" therefore
ensures the subordination of all fragmentary interests to
those of the transcendental totality.

It is in this context that we must view contemporary
efforts by city planners to gentrify and redevelop downtown
as a deliberate attempt to regulate and control racial differences in terms of the city's visual space. One reason for
doing this is related to the idea that difference is threatening
and evokes conflict. Hence, the restoration of a city's architectural history is meant "to invoke a past existing only in
the realm of the imaginary, eliciting from viewers a nostalgia—bound up with objects—for a flawless environment"
(Deutsche, 1991d:160). To preserve this illusion, cities can

only be constructed in terms of expelling the differences and conflicts within it. In fact, celebratory accounts of real estate or the state-sponsored plans to restore the past architectural heritage of cities are not "confined to describing the historical character of individual restorations nor even to insinuating that such projects reinstate the pleasures of some distant aristocratic era" (Deutsche, 1991d:160). Instead, the euphemisms of urban restoration projects have as much or more to do with the constructing of ideological consent against what is perceived as disruptive and threatening forms of difference:

> [Celebratory accounts] intimate, more equivocally, that projects undertaken in the name of preservation represent advances in a struggle to restore—against disruptive forces—a model city from the more remote past, one that is harmonious in its entirety. By alluding to far-reaching restorative goals and in the process, summoning up a past that never existed, the newly conservative urban aesthetic is able to explain its own contradictions between, for one, its preservationist rhetoric and real destructive acts. (Deutsche, 1991d:160)

Finally, this preservationist rhetoric has been really destructive to black urban settlements, particularly when the task of architectural redevelopment has been to maintain ideological stability. By evoking the nostalgic image of the harmonious city, preservationists are able to rationalize ideologically that the dispersal of black settlements or ghettos from downtown is essential for the re-establishment of harmony. Because, unlike the early city planners who believed that the decay of the physical urban environment caused the moral and behavioral decay of European immigrants, today's urban planners argue that it is black American culture itself which is mostly responsible for the physical and moral deterioration of American cities. In the contemporary city, the urban has become a metaphor for race, for black people. The urban form, particularly its representation through the image of redevelopment or gentrification, is understood in relation to a politics of racial difference. That is to say, the urban spaces of black Americans in a white supremacist urban culture are racialized by constructing binary oppositions, contrasting black spaces with white ones.

M. Christine Boyer argues that space in the city has increasingly become fragmented, and that because of this, it "is hierarchicalized into high/low ensembles—luxury areas, middle-class residential neighborhoods, historic centers, profitable areas—which are juxtaposed against the abandoned areas of the city, its slums, immigrant districts and poorer sections" (1990:102). It is in this context that the living spaces of blacks are juxtaposed with the living spaces of whites. However, I would argue that the hierarchicalizing of the black and white living spaces must be understood in terms of how power passes itself off as embodied in the "normal," rather than the "superior." In other words, the symbolic representation of the living spaces of whites as "normal" is always constructed around a politics and language of difference. That is, the textual and visual representation of white living spaces as normal assumes that black living spaces are *not* normal. As already discussed, power passes itself as embodied in the normal. According to Richard Dyer, "This is common to all forms of power, but it works in peculiarly seductive ways with whiteness, because of the way it seems rooted, in commonsense thought, in things other than ethnic difference" (1988:20). This means that a pedagogy of place has to take up difference in relation to a politics of race and ethnicity; it must address the issue of whites colonizing definitions of normal in relation to the material landscape of the city.

This normalizing of difference in a white supremacist urban culture means that the racializing of black living spaces gets constructed around a notion of irrationality, disordered and uncivilized behavior, and white living spaces around rationality and ordered and civilized behavior. In *Neighborhood Revitalization* Philip Clay's discussion about gentrifiying neighborhoods is informed by this binary logic:

At the positive end . . . are members of the "civil class," whose attitudes and behaviors are based on the assumption that the individual good, and hence the neighborhood good, is enhanced by submitting to social norms. At the other extreme are members of the "uncivil class." Their behavior and attitudes reflect no acceptance of norms beyond those imperfectly specified by civil and criminal law. Their attitudes may range from indifference to social norms to hostility toward any collective definition of behavior. (1978:37-38)

This particular representation of gentrifying neighborhoods is rooted in an image of the city as an "urban frontier" or "urban wilderness." Within this image, the "civil class" is portrayed as "urban pioneers" who bring "civilization" to the wilderness (Smith, Neil, 1992:69-75). For example, upon the completion of a redevelopment project two blocks west of Time Square, the real estate section of the *New York Times* announced, "The Taming of the Wild Wild West." The article goes on to say, "The trailblazers have done their work: West 42nd street has been tamed, domesticated, and polished into the most exciting, freshest, most energetic new neighborhood in all of New York" (Smith, Neil, 1992:69). According to Neil Smith, the frontier motif encodes the entire urban environment, from the names of upscale apartments, condominiums, speciality stores, and galleries to urban fashion and furniture (1992:69-71). This frontier motif combines the city with the desert, evoking for the present past images of the white man conquering the "wild Indians" (1992:72).

Through frontier imagery artists romanticize the ghetto. Quoting one local art critic, Smith states, "One must realize that East village or the Lower East Side is more than a geographical location—it is a state of mind" (1992:76). In response to this Smith says that "[o]nly in the Lower East Side do art critics celebrate 'minifestivals of the slum art'; only here do artists cherish 'a basic ghetto material—the ubiquitous brick'; and only here would the art entourage admit to being 'captivated by the liveliness of ghetto culture'" (1992:76). Smith, however, points out that frontier danger is the other side of this romance: "Frontier danger permeates the very art itself. As one apologist gushed, the scene is ruled by the 'law of the jungle' and the new art exudes 'savage energy'; neo-primitivist art, depicting black-figured urban natives running wild in the streets, presumably expressed this savage energy" (1992:77).

Underlying this is the white racist perception that blacks are irrational, disordered and uncivilized. "Blacks are constantly constituted by Whites as 'the fantasy of a fantasy—not cold, pure, clean, efficient, industrious, frugal, rational but rather warm, dirty, sloppy, feckless, lazy, improvident and irrational, all those traits that are associated with Blackness, odor, and sensuality" (Young, 1991:193). In fact, these traits contrast strongly with the traits of the "White City"—orderliness, cleanliness, and whiteness—and therefore with the aesthetic qualities of neoclassical architecture, such as order, proportion, rhythm, equilibrium, purity, and harmony (Boyer, 1986). In this context the "pleasure of looking" at neoclassical architecture is mediated by white fantasies about blacks. This suggests that the gentrification (architectural redevelopment) of the city is mediated by white supremacist ideology.

Gentrification of the city cannot be explained solely with reference to the redevelopment of space; it also involves the image of redevelopment. From this vantage point, gentrification is seen more in terms of how it "constructs the built environment as a medium, one we literally inhabit, that monopolizes popular memory by controlling the representation of its own history" (Deutsche, 1991a:176). This silences and marginalizes the historical and cultural, but everyday, meanings that blacks give to their particular place in the built environment. The architecture of redevelopment allows mainstream whites to represent their own history as universal. This implies a "representation of redevelopment" that is based on an essentialist discourse that believes that the beauty and utility of the "white city" is inherently functional to the creation of "public" spaces.

Furthermore, the functional logic of this discourse has permitted the white middle class, through urban planning, design, and architecture, to operate in the "name of the public" as a homogenizing force within the city. That is to say that "the ideology of function obscures the conflictual manner in which cities are actually defined and used, repudiating the very existence of groups who counter dominant uses of space" (Deutsche, 1991a:160). The consequence of this essentialist representation of redevelopment by urban planners, designers, and architects is that it literally deterritorializes huge numbers of black residents, "causing the atrophy of public space into private or state-controlled areas that tolerate little resistance to approved uses" (Deutsche, 1991a:174). Even as the provision of "public" space by redevelopment projects is dubbed as a triumph for the public, the deterritorialization of black residents destroys the very material basis of their public life. The threat to black public space has to be linked to the withdrawal of physical space from which blacks can organize their experience into a politics and culture of resistance. Roslyan Deutsche in agreement writes,

> What is threatened with extinction is the territorial conditions for situating a public sphere—at once a concrete spatial form and a social arena of radically democratic political debate—are seriously undermined. The public sphere is in this sense what one might call the factory of politics—its site of production proposing the establishment of a truly public sphere that opposes the exclusionary rights of private property and state intervention. (1991a:174-75)

Chapter Four

Conclusion: Toward a Pedagogy of Place for Black Urban Struggle

Introduction

What possibilities does critical pedagogy have for constructing "a pedagogy of place" for black urban struggle? An answer to this question must begin by addressing the relationship between urban struggles and the production of urban meanings. Urban conflicts can be seen as antagonism over the construction and interpretation of the city as a myth, which in turn have implications for who and how the material landscape of the city is designed (Castells, 1983; Davis, 1992). That is to say, urban conflicts are about the representation of the city, but more important, who represents the city, who produces its myths (Dennis, 1990). Mike Davis in *City of Quartz* is interested in the mythography of Los Angeles, particularly "the history of culture produced about Los Angeles—especially where that has become a material force in the city's actual evolution" (1990:20). He points out that since the 1930s cultural intellectuals such as architects, designers, artists, filmmakers, writers, and cultural theorists, at the invitation and sponsorship of the largest land developers and bankers, have played a major role in constructing the image of Los Angeles (1990:20). It is important to recognize that these images "are powerful ideological instruments of real politics because they are turned from "vision statements" into "general plans" for the expansion of capital in the urban" (Keith, 1993:112). Keith states: "The lofty [images] serve as a shield behind which the destruction of neighborhoods, gentrification and displacement occurs" (1993:112).

It is this context that necessitates the development of a pedagogy of place for black urban struggle that incorporates the contributions of critical pedagogy. In what follows, I will begin to address this issue by referring to some of the major points raised in the proceeding chapters. In Chapter 2, I argued that a sense of meaninglessness and hopelessness is becoming pervasive in contemporary black life (West, 1991b; hooks and West, 1991). For the most part, the exotic interests of the white middle class consumer culture in popular black culture have been responsible for breaking down the structure of meaning in black urban communities, because mainstream white consumer culture has commodified and reified black popular culture, thereby detaching black culture from its historical and social references.

This detachment speaks to how "race" as defined in relation to blackness and black people has become in the white supremacist culture of the city a metaphor for the urban, that is, a metaphor that signifies simultaneously the pleasures and dangers of blackness in the city. Elizabeth Wilson attributes this to the postmodern culture of the post-industrial corporate city, which she argues "perceives all experience in aesthetic terms (1991:136). However, what is important to Wilson about this is that in the postmodern city the "unpleasurable" is aestheticized to obtain a perverse pleasure. She states: "Horror, fear and ugliness are aestheticized, and thus become easier to live with, at least for the new urban aesthete, the voyeur. Postmoderism thus expresses an urban sensibility, although a perverse one" (1991:136). Cross and Keith also call attention to how in the postmodern city "ethnicity is celebrated in the collage of the exotic cultural pick-and-mix, while race remains taboo, and is anything but playful" (1993:8). In doing so, mainstream white consumer culture reappropriates the categories "race" and "urban" to signify the pleasures and dangers of blackness, controlling and regulating black cultural identity and how blacks define and use urban space. This has implications for black urban struggle in that image makers in the postmodern city tend to aestheticize experiences instead of responding morally or emotionally. They act to mask mainstream white privilege and corporate power in the city (Wilson, 1991:150).

A way to begin to think about these issues in relation to a pedagogy of place for black urban struggle is to situate black popular culture within the context of black city life. The Twentieth-Century city has been one of the main sources of meaning for contemporary black popular culture. And at the same time that the city has contributed to its production, black popular culture has shaped the production of urban meanings. The city for blacks has been an important site for place making, for producing black culture and black identity. The concept of place making is used here to denote that places are significant because we assign values to them in relation to our cultural projects: "Place is the fusion of space and experience, a space filled with meaning, a source of identity" (Friedland, 1992:14).

In *City and the Grassroots*, Manuel Castells asserts that "cultural identity [is] associated with and organized around a specific territory" (1983:14). Elaborating on this point, Brett Williams observes that dense living in the city has made black American culture seem vibrant: "Through the work of the street [blacks] build a vivid detailed repertoire of biographical, historical, and everyday knowledge about community life" (1988:4). In addition, the meanings and uses that blacks assign to their specific territory are defined around a popular memory of black rural southern culture: "Through the shared lore of alley gardens, through the exchange of medicines and delicacies, through fishing and feasting among metropolitan kin, and in visits, exchanges, and the construction of an alternative economy with relatives that bring Carolina harvest to the city" (Williams, 1988:3).

By producing urban meanings that recall popular memories of black rural southern culture, blacks have been able to construct alternative identities and relationships based on ties of friendship, family, history, and place. Blacks therefore define and use urban space to renegotiate an oppositional identity which knits together neighbors and draws families together across the city" (Williams, 1988:3). Renegotiating their identities as blacks is linked to place making. It involves the production of public spheres, which bell hooks refers to as "homeplace," "site[s] where one could confront the issue of humanization, where one could resist" (hooks, 1990:42). As spaces of care and nurturance, homeplaces, according to hooks, are where "all black people could be subjects, not objects, where we could be affirmed in our minds and hearts despite poverty, hardship, and deprivation, where we could restore to ourselves dignity denied us on the outside in the public world" (1990:42). The black public sphere is therefore the basis for building a community of resistance. Refering to the public sphere of marginalized or subaltern communities Nancy Fraser comes to the same conclusion:

> Subaltern counterpublics have a dual character. On the one hand, they function as spaces of withdrawal and regroupment; on the other hand, they also function as bases and training grounds for agitational activities directed toward wider publics. It is precisely in the dialectic between these two functions that their emancipatory potential resides. (1991:69)

It is this dual character of counterpublics that provides the necessary conditions for developing oppositional identities.

The public sphere is not only an arena for the formation of discursive opinion; it is an arena for the formation and enactment of social identities; it is the arena that allows one to speak in one's own voice (Fraser, 1991:69). Public spheres are therefore culturally specific institutions, which, according to Fraser, include various social geographies of urban space (1991:69).

The social geography of urban space is characterized by public spaces in the city that are positioned unequally in relation to one another with respect to power. The concept of power is key to interpreting this positionality, to understanding how public spaces relate to one another in the context of the city. In particular, if power is linked to the production of urban meaning, then those public spaces located at the center of city life dominate its meaning, and in so doing define the cultural and political terrain in which marginalized public spaces, in this case black public spaces, resist, form alternative identities, and make culture in the city. In this way, the physical space of the black ghetto is a public sphere, a culturally specific institution. Because inner-city blacks live on the margins of white supremacist domination and privilege, they have no other alternative than to struggle for the transformation of their places on the margin into spaces of cultural resistance. Michael Keith and Steve Pile observe that "for those who have no place that can be safely called home, there must be a struggle for a place to be" (1993:5). This is why bell hooks argues that historically, "African American people believed that the construction of a homeplace, however fragile and tenuous (the slave hut, the wooden shack) had a radical political dimension" (1990:42). What this indicates is that the struggle by blacks for place is bound up with their identity politics. The problem with this is that if black identity is viewed as fixed, perceived in biologistic terms and not as a social construction, then the meanings attached to place are perceived as being fixed. In a white supremacist culture that equates race with being black, the meanings and uses that blacks attach to a place are believed to be derived from their biology, from their nature. As a particular kind of place, the category "urban" has been inscribed with racial meaning; it has operated as a racial metaphor for black. What this means is that black cultural politics in relation to place making should avoid essentialist constructions of blackness and black identity when defining and using their public spaces in the city. If they do not, they risk reinforcing white supremacist stereotypes that rationalize redevelopment practices that displace blacks from their public spaces.

It is imperative, then, that a pedagogy of place maintain or establish the necessary conditions for the development of black public spheres within the "ghetto territory." To do this, it should draw on the tradition of critical pedagogy. Henry Giroux argues that in relation to producing counterpublic spheres, critical pedagogy must be seen "as having an important role in the struggle of oppressed groups to reclaim the ideological and material conditions for organizing their own experiences" (1983:237). Critical pedagogy in the context of black city life has a crucial role to play in the production of counterpublics, in constructing political and cultural practices that organize human experiences enabling individuals to interpret social reality in liberating ways. However, for a "pedagogy of place" this must be understood in terms of establishing pedagogical conditions that enable blacks in the city to critically interpret how dominant definitions and uses of urban space regulate and control how they organize their identity around territory, and the consequences of this for black urban resistance.

Preceding the "Great Black Migration" to northern and midwestern cities, urban areas were mainly white. After the formation of large black urban settlements resulting from the migration, the urban was described metaphorically as a jungle, as being dominated by bestial, predatory values. With the mass migration of southern blacks to cities in the north, the "city as a jungle" began to operate as a racist metaphor to describe inner-city blacks (Gilroy, 1991:228). "It has contributed," observes Paul Gilroy, "to contemporary definitions of 'race,' particularly those which highlight the sup-

posed primitivism and violence of black residents in inner-
city areas" (1991:229). The metaphorical construction of the
urban around "race" is of particular significance given that in
a white supremacist culture that identities race with being
black and not being white the urban becomes another way to
signify the "evils" of blackness and black people. This can be
seen in relation to current discussions about poor black
urban families and the rise in black inner-city homicides,
particularly in relation to black males.

Before directly commenting on this, I want to first make
the argument that the ideological construction of the "city
as a jungle" is related to the idea that the culture of the city
is based on so-called black street culture. For example, the
motif that is most prevalent in Levi blue jeans ads is "street
cool," which suggests a romantic view of ghetto life.
Implied in such a view "is a conception about acting in public spaces and how blacks accomplish this" (Goldman and
Papson, 1992:83). The subtext of Levi ads is that "black
males move without inhibition to the rhythm of the street
because [t]hey signify soul, movement, expressiveness, the
body unencumbered by tight, stiff middle-classness"
(Goldman and Papson, 1992:83). Accompanying this is
Levi's exotic use of black urban music to signify the body,
hence sexuality; it is appropriated to express the physical
sensuality and movement associated with jeans among
youth. Thus, by stylizing and softening the black ghetto,
Levi commercials detach black culture from the pain and
anguish of black city life:

> In relation to the street itself, Levi's images are
> incomplete—they have been purged of poverty and
> its ill effects, streetpeople, violence, petty crime. . . .
> Levi's romanticizes poverty—gives it authenticity
> by cleaning it up. In fact, this ad is only real in rela-
> tion to what has previously been seen on television
> and in the mass media. Relative to the street, Levi's
> account is not hyperreal, but stylized. (Goldman and
> Papson, 1992:83)

By separating black popular urban culture from the harsh realities of black city life mainstream white consumer culture silences and marginalizes black narratives and stories of racial exclusion and racial humiliation, of daily pain and suffering experienced due to white supremacist practices in the city. It is in this context that black popular urban culture is in part an expression of the day-to-day life of inner-city blacks.

One way to begin to understand the day-to-day life of urban blacks is by looking at how the place-making practices of mainstream white institutions in the city dismantle the living spaces, and therefore public spaces or homeplaces, of inner-city blacks. This means that to address in pedagogical terms black life in the city, critical educators must have an understanding of how mainstream whites in the city—through developers, landlords, politicians, banks, and corporations—texually and visually represent space in their image of redevelopment. In an effort to attract middleclass whites and corporations to the city, urban planners, designers, and architects are employed by cities to construct a visual image of the city representing social stability. Through the restoration of neoclassical architectural forms the city is represented as harmonious. Planners believe that the aesthetics of neoclassical architecture signify orderliness, cleanliness, and whiteness, which are all articulated with civic ideals, such as national unity and national pride.

By evoking these civic ideals, neoclassical architecture is used as a way to "restore tradition" in the city. In this sense, architectural redevelopment or gentrification is tied to a nostalgia for the past. Here, however, the use of nostalgia defines and represents "tradition" as "heritage." This nostalgia for "tradition" is used to delineate 'us' from 'them,' reinforcing old hierarchies of race (Levitas, 1990). From this point of view, the urban "place-making" practices of blacks are seen as a threat to "tradition" because of the different uses and values assigned to place as discussed above. The argument is that in "making place," the social uses and cultural values assigned by blacks to their living spaces are thought to perpetuate all those qualities associated with "blackness" in the white racist imagination, such as disorderliness, filthiness, ugliness, and irrationality. This is in contrast to those qualities asso ated with "whiteness" that are believed to be embodied in neoclassical architecture, such as order, purity, beauty, and rationality. It is in this context that neoclassical architecture is thought to contain essential and universal meanings (Boyer, 1986:66). The implied assumption is that the beauty and utility of neoclassical architecture is inherently functional to the creation of public spaces.

It is important to remember that black public spaces in the city have historically been centered around daily survival; it is these "spaces of survival" that serve as public spaces where black people develop self-definitions or identities that are linked to a consciousness of solidarity and to a politics of resistance. Sivanandan implies this when stating, "Regulated to a concrete ghetto and deprived of basic amenities and services, jobless for the most part . . . the inhabitants came together to create a life for themselves." Continuing this same point later, Sivanandan observes, "They set up a nursery, provide meals and a meeting place, establish a recreation centre for youth and build up in the process, a political culture." He concludes by saying that these spaces of survival "were prefigured in the black struggles of the 1960s and 1970s" (1990:52). For the Black Power movement of the 1960s and 1970s, the city was perceived as the place in which blacks could form what Sivanandan calls "organic communities of resistance." James Jenning argues that in the city black political activism equates empowerment with control of land in the black urban communities, and that this notion of empowerment surpasses affirmative action, job discrimination, or school integration (1990:120). Cynthia Hamilton argues that the significance of land for the development of oppositional political communities can constitute a threat to the dominant social order and result in the "manipulation of space" to remove certain populations from the spaces they inhabit.

In South Africa, "forced removals" are responsible
for the relocation of millions to the remote home-
lands. In Guatemala, the government is building
model villages which grew out of army efforts in the
1980s to control rural communities by displacing
the population and forcing resettlements. . . . In the
U.S., we have our own version of forced removal and
resettlement, our own overt manipulation of behavior through spatial transformations. The form that
this relocation and restructuring has taken is urban
renewal and community development. The relocation and removal has had a very important consequence in the curtailing of political organization.
(Hamilton, 1991:28)

How do mainstream white urban institutions legitimate
or rationalize the removal of black populations living in the
city? My argument is that the category space is culturally
produced and ordered. According to David Goldberg,
"Spatial distinctions like 'West' and 'East' are racialized in
their conception and application" (1993:183). This for
Goldberg means that "racial categories have been variously
spatialized more or less since their inception into conti-
nental divides, national localities, and geographical regions"
(1993:183). What is suggested is that through the racializing
of populations, the spaces they inhabit are also racialized;
therefore, in a white supremacist society like the United
States, the spaces of racialized populations, black, Latino,
and Asian, are differentiated from the spaces of the non-
racialized population, in this case mainstream white. It is by
discursively constructing populations and their spaces as
racialized that mainstream white institutions in the city
legitimate the removal and colonizing of the inner city. In
many ways, the equating of the urban with "race" has
allowed white mainstream institutions to define "urban
problems"—single-parent households, violence, poverty,
joblessness, drugs—as the problem of race, and therefore
the problem of blacks. In doing this, black spaces in the city

are represented as "spaces of pathology," as "spaces of disorder," without any consideration of how the colonizing of space by mainstream white institutions in the city removed and destroyed the communal living spaces, the "homeplaces" of urban blacks.

The urban renewal programs in the United States described the removal and destruction of black public spaces as "slum clearance." Goldberg argues that by definition the "slum" means filthy, foul smelling, wretched, rancorous, uncultivated, and lacking care" (1993:191). But in terms of the racial slum, he says it "is doubly determined, for the metaphorical stigma of a black blotch on the cityscape bears the added connotations of moral degeneracy, natural inferiority, and repulsiveness" (Goldberg, 1993:192). In the late 1950s and 1960s the U.S. urban renewal programs focused on the removal and destruction of black public spaces in the name of slum clearance. This process occurred simultaneously with the expansion of black northern urban settlements, during the second "Great Black Migration." The conceptualization and application of "slum clearance" originated with the removal of Africans from their land by colonial administrations to make way for European cities in Africa. Fearful that Africans would pollute the living spaces of European settlers colonial administrators segregated them.

> Uncivilized Africans, it was claimed, suffered urbanization as a pathology of disorder and degeneration of their traditional tribal life. To prevent their pollution contaminating European city dwellers and services, the idea of sanitation and public health was invoked first as the legal path to remove blacks to separate locations at the city limits and then as a principle for sustaining permanent segregation. (Goldberg, 1994:190)

In postwar Euro-American cities urban planning too produced a racialized divided cityscape. Urban renewal programs in the United States were designed around a twofold strategy, according to Goldberg. The primary motivation behind both strategies was white fear of black encroachment into white neighborhoods. One part of the strategy was to clear the slums and to rehouse the black population into towering public housing projects. The idea was to "reproduce the inner-city slum on a smaller scale." Goldberg describes this process as "warehousing the racially marginalized" (1993:191). The second part of the urban renewal strategy was to clear the slum and on a massive scale "remove the cities' racial poor with no plans to rehouse them" (Goldberg, 1993:191). The idea here was to force a "large proportion of the racialized poor to settle for slum conditions marginalized at the city limits" (Goldberg, 1993:191). This was described as "Negro Removal." Another term used by federal urban renewal programs, particularly in the 1960s and 1970s was "spatial deconcentration." As mentioned in Chapter 3, geographer Harold Rose points out in "The Future of the Black Ghetto" (1982) that in the future "ghetto centers will essentially be confined to a selected set of suburban ring communities. [There] appears to be little concern regarding the social and economic implications associated with the present spatial reorganization upon the future of urban blacks, . . . or for that matter upon the future of the city" (cited from Smith, Neil, 1992:92-93).

In the context of a white supremacist society, the culture of race and racism has much significance in terms of the spatial organization of cities in the United States. For mainstream white urban institutions the spatial "regeneration" of the city is linked to the discursive representation and control of racial differences. Goldberg points out that "regeneration" is constructed from a notion of "degeneration." From the viewpoint of white supremacist culture, the racialized urban poor are represented as "degenerate" and subsequently regressive. That is to say, the "slums" emerge because the racialized urban poor are perceived as naturally incapable of living in the modern city. "Races accordingly have their proper or natural places, geographically and biologically. Displaced from their proper or normal class, national, or ethnic positions in the social and ultimately urban setting, a 'Native' or 'Negro' would generate pathologies." Stratified by race and class, the modern city becomes a testing ground of survival, of racialized power and control (Goldberg, 1993:200). The Enlightment ideal of the modern city as a place of individualism, economic opportunity, and material progress implies that the racialized urban poor live in slums because they do not have the innate qualities needed to survive in the modern world, in the bourgeois city. Regeneration therefore is linked to the "spiritual and physical renewal" of the city for those naturally fit to live in it. Goldberg goes on to say that "gentrification is the form of regeneration that most readily defines the postmodern city" (1993:201).

In *Unheavenly City* Banfield argues that "black slums" are not the result of "racial prejudice" because "discrimination was not the main obstacle in the way of Irish, the Italians, the Jews and others that have made it. Nor is it the main one of the Negro" (Banfield, 1968:78). Banfield then goes on to say, "If [the Negro] lives in a neighborhood that is all-black, the reason is not white prejudice. This physical separation may arise from [the Negro] having cultural characteristics that make him an undesirable neighbor" (1968:79). He also writes, "Impulse governs his behavior, either because he cannot discipline himself to sacrifice a present for a future satisfaction or because he has no sense of the future. He is therefore radically improvident: whatever he cannot use immediately he considers valueless. His bodily needs (especially sex) and his taste for 'action' take precedence over everything else" (1974:61). Banfield further suggests that "to a greater extent [the slum] is an expression of his tastes and style of life" (1974:71), implying that "the slum has its own subculture" (1974:71). Hence, for Banfield, "[t]he subcultural norms and values of the slum are reflected in poor sanitation and health practices, deviant behavior and often a real lack of interests in formal education" (1974:71). In addition, by claiming that the "subculture of the slum" rested on the premise that the Negro's bodily needs (especially sex) and his taste for "action" took precedence over everything else, Banfield moves to describe the urban riots as "outbreaks of animal spirits" (1968:297). This view of the urban uprisings was implicit in his essay "Rioting for Fun and for Profit."

Others have used this to call for the physical displacement of blacks from the city. Charles Murray, the ideologue of the New Right's antiwelfare policies and author of *Losing Ground* which was dubbed by Ronald Reagan as the "bible" of welfare reform, wants to restore the right of landlords and employers to discriminate—"without having to justify their arbitrariness" (Davis, 1992:178) "Only by letting, 'like-minded people . . . control and shape their small worlds,' and letting landlords pursue their natural instincts 'to let good tenants be and to evict bad ones,' can the larger part of urban America find its golden age of harmonious, self-regulating communities" (cited in Davis, 1992:178). Murray concludes by saying, "If the result of implementing those policies is to concentrate the bad apples into a few hyperviolent, antisocial neighborhoods, so be it" (cited in Davis, 1992:178). It is, in fact, this particular attitude that has lead to the actual dispersing of black urban settlements from downtown. David Reed argues for instance that HUD's "spatial deconcentration" program was established in the wake of the black rebellions of the 1960s as a means of dispersing blacks to remote suburban neighborhoods where geographic isolation would prevent them from organizing (1981:ii).

In addition to being spatially excluded from downtown, the dispersion of the black population to near suburbs has also been increasingly complimented with police repression and surveillance. Mike Davis, in "Fortress L.A.: The Militarization of Urban Space," discusses how efforts to criminalize inner-city communities, such as the "war" on drugs and gangs have served as a pretext for police departments to experiment with community blockades. For example, in Los Angeles, "narcotic enforcement zones" provided the LAPD with an excuse to conduct massive illegal searches and arrests under its Operation Hammer program. Comparing this to the West Bank strategy Davis writes:

> As the HAMMER mercilessly pounded away at southcentral's mean streets, it became increasingly apparent that its principle catch consisted of drunks, delinquent motorists and teenage curfew violators (offenders only by virtue of the selective application of curfews to non-Anglo neighborhoods). By 1990 the combined forces of the LAPD and the Sheriffs (implementing there own street saturation strategy) had picked up as many as 50,000 suspects. Even allowing for a percentage of Latino detainees, this remains an astonishing figure considering there are only 100,000 Black youths in Los Angeles. In some highly touted sweeps, moreover, as many as 90 percent of detained suspects have been released without charges. (1990:277)

In U.S. cities the criminalization of black youth has acted to racialize and therefore demonize the public spaces of blacks in the city. The criminalization accomplished is by using racist stereotypes that suggest that most or all black youth are members of gangs. The Urban Strategies Group in Los Angeles commented on how L.A. District Attorney Ira Reiner in a report concluded that "some of the most troubling data to emerge from this study concern the extraordinary percentage of young Black males who show up in gang data bases. The police has identified almost half of all Black men in Los Angeles County between the ages of 21 and 24 as gang members" (1992:7). The Urban Stategies Group points out that in fact, "the police simply equated being in a 'database' that they created with being in a gang."

By the assumed association with gangs, black youth are believed to be heavily involved in drug trafficking, and it is also assumed that most of the violence results from that involvement. The findings of a study conducted by Malcolm Klein, Cherly Maxson, and Lea Cunningham of the University of Southern California directly contradict the

gang-drug-violence connection. They found that "gang violence is primarily related to gang issues, such as rivalries,
not to drugs. . . . We find no evidence of spiralling effects of
drug involvement in homicides between the mid and later
year of the 1980s. Again we conclude that concern for specific gang/drug/violence connections has been overstated, at
least in [south central] Los Angeles" (Urban Strategies
Group, 1992:7). The Strategies Group argues that linking
black youth with gangs, drugs, and violence has "create[d] a
mandate for police brutality and abuse. The outcome of all
this is that criminalization acts a process of racialization"
(Keith, 1993).

    This racialization of crime explains the increasing repres-
sion and surveillance of the black community found by the
Sentencing Project (1991), which concluded that one out of
every two black men will be arrested in his lifetime and that
the incarceration rate for black people in the United States is
four times as high as that of black people in South Africa.
Interestingly, while remaining more or less constant from
1925 until 1971, U.S. incarceration rates since 1972 have
tripled. This upward spiral coincides with the urban rebellions, which were an expression of black resistance to the
dismantling of black settlements due to the aggressive urban
renewal initiatives being sponsored by local governments.

    In *City and the Grassroots*, Manuel Castells argues that
although the 1968 Kerner Commission was correct that
poverty has been an underlying condition of the African
American community, the Commission was mistaken to
assume that it was the immediate cause of the urban rebel-
lion (1983:52). Instead, he argues that the cause of the urban
rebellions was associated more with "the size of the black
population; and the location of this population in the
Northern regions of America" (1983:52). In addition to this,
he believes that the severity of the riots had much to do
with the housing crisis and with aggressive urban renewal
policies, particularly within a context of police harassment
and undemocratic local government (1983:52). However,
the urban riots were not simply a response to the "physical"

dismantling of black settlements. They were just as much or more a reaction to the consequent disruption of black civil society.

Since cultural identity is associated with and organized around territory, dismantling disrupts black identity formation by destroying the material basis of the black public sphere. By withdrawing the public sphere's physical space, urban blacks are less able to sustain the networks of family and friends necessary for organizing their experiences into a collective identity. Referring to the public sphere, Alexander Kluge in a similar vein states, "The loss of land also means a loss of community because if there is no land on which [dominated groups] may assemble, it is no longer possible to develop community" (1991-82:213). The "redevelopment of space" by dominant interests in the city threatens the very material basis of black public life; that is, private use of public space is literally deterrioralizing the black community. Or in the words of Rosalyn Deutsche, "The territorial conditions for situating a public sphere—at once a concrete spatial form and a social arena of radically democratic political debate—are seriously [being] undermined" (1990:175). It is in the context of deterritoralization that the "black public sphere" is being destroyed and black civil society shattered.

Nevertheless, the withdrawal of physical space is not the only threat to the formation of a collective black identity. Equally threatening is how "the architecture of redevelopment or gentrification constructs the built environment as a medium that monopolizes popular memory by controlling the representation of its own history [in urban space]" (Deutsche, 1991d:176). Put another way, mainstream white culture's image of redevelopment and its celebration of neoclassical architecture silences and marginalizes the popular stories, narratives, and memories of black place making, of black life in the city. This is significant in that these popular stories and narratives provide black urban culture with a popular vernacular. The implication is that when black urban culture is detached from its popular vernacular, from its stories and narratives of place making, blacks have less opportunity to associate their pain and anguish—unemployment, police harassment, homelessness, and hunger—with redevelopment.

It is in this context that I argue for the necessity of developing a pedagogy of place. Such a pedagogy should focus on how the loss of place-making memories by blacks is connected to how mainstream meanings and uses of urban space are naturalized by the deployment of an ideology of function, which mistakenly assumes that mainstream white definitions and uses are inherently functional to the creation of public spaces in cities. Architectural redevelopment or gentrification is believed to be functional, because it purports to "humanize" or "beautify" the environment, supposedly enhancing public use and viewer perception of the city. Also of concern is how the ideology of function obscures the role of conflict, domination, and resistance in defining what constitutes the public, and subsequently how public spaces in the city should be used and assigned meaning. A pedagogy of place must therefore facilitate blacks critically coming to voice about their own popular memories and histories of place making in the city. What this means is that black popular urban culture must be recontextualized in terms of black struggles around territory and place (Castells, 1983). This is crucial because mainstream white consumer culture detaches black popular urban culture by exoticizing black city life. Neil Smith elaborates on how artists' romanticizing the ghetto has lead to the trivializing of urban conflict:

> Especially in the context of intense media emphasis on crime and drugs in the area, the artistic invocation of danger is usually too oblique to highlight the sharp conflicts over gentrification. . . . The world's cooptation of violent urban imagery generally trivializes real struggles and projects a sense of danger that is difficult to take seriously. Social conflict is recast as artistic spectacle danger as ambience. With the rapidity of openings and closings, moving and renamings, gentrification and decay, a landscape of happy vio-

lence becomes the stage for a dynamic and breathless new form of geographical performance art. (1992:77)

Another closely related concern of a pedagogy of place is with the impact of mainstream white consumer culture on black cultural identity. One major concern is that blacks through packaged and commodified stimulation have become addicted to the seductive images of mainstream white consumer culture—comfort, convenience, machismo, femininity, violence, and sexual stimulation (West, 1991b:224). According to West, a "market morality" is being created "where one understands oneself as living to consume" (1991:10). He says that this "morality is creating a 'market culture' where one's communal and political identity is shaped by the adoration and cultivation of images, celebrityhood, and visibility" (1992:95). Bell hooks believes that the pervasiveness of the culture of consumption in black life "undermines our capacity to experience community" (1992:10). This is of major concern given that cultural identity is associated with territory. This is also of significance given that racist imagination of mainstream white consumer culture has reappropriated black culture to construct "commodified" pleasure. In this way, black culture has become increasingly focused inward and individualistic. Black culture's commodification has made it less concerned with joy, that is, with "those nonmarket values—love, care, kindness, service, solidarity, the struggle for justice—values that provide the possibility of bringing people together" (Dent, 1992:1).

This being the case, blacks have become complicitous in wanting to convert the public spaces of the ghetto into private spaces of consumption. The building of public housing, community libraries, community-owned and managed cooperatives, cultural centers, and schools are subordinated to shopping malls and private homeownership. This is done under the pretext that this will bring social stability to black inner-city neighborhoods. John Logan and Harvey Molotch show how this point of view dominates black community-based organizations:

The temptation to partake in the social "upgrading" of a neighborhood is in the context of the tough problems of crime, poverty, and funding crisis, the sincere yearning of the "decent" residents is seductive; and it is easy to exclude the winos, homeless, and hoodlums as a constituency. The most efficient way to solve the neighborhood problems is perhaps through a triage system in which the best-off receive attention, the poorest are abandoned, and the middle receive the most. Raising the neighborhood's social class, even if only by a little, enables a community organization to show progress in cleaning up the neighborhood. (Logan and Molotch, 1987:145)

Underlying this is the belief that the middle-class built environment—shopping malls, single-family homes, luxury apartments and condominiums, boutiques, specialty food stores, restaurants, historic centers—forms the basis of a "stable" community. What is meant by "a stable community" is that the public spaces of the city are organized around upscale consumer-oriented entertainment and leisure. In fact, this suggests that this particular built environment corresponds with the lifestyle of the middle class, a lifestyle that Thorstein Veblen argued is defined by conspicuous consumption and conspicuous leisure. The point is that private consumption is being viewed by blacks as the way to use and define public space in the ghetto territory. In support of this view, blacks become complicitous in silencing and marginalizing their own stories and narratives about place making. The result is that blacks are rendered less able to develop oppositional public spheres.

Towards a Pedagogy of Place for Black Urban Resistance

In the context of the inner city, a pedagogy of place must be linked to black urban struggle. It must be involved in the building of oppositional public spaces, to forming spaces of care and nurturance or, as bell hooks would say, "home-places." However, for black urban communities to build oppositional public spaces or homeplaces a pedagogy of place must first work with them in redefining the nature of black urban struggle. One of the major contradictions of black urban struggle is its demand for redevelopment or gentrification *without* displacement. Even when blacks have control over the redevelopment process many blacks are still displaced. Black urban struggles overlook how the very notion of redevelopment or gentrification itself is premised on the racialization of certain urban populations, mainly nonwhite populations—in this case, blacks—to legitimate their forced removal or warehousing in the city. I discussed above how Goldberg points out that notions like "degeneration" and "regeneration" are informed by a racial subtext. He shows how "degeneration" is connoted with "blacks" and "slums"; "regeneration" with progress and renewal; and whites with the process of "gentrification."

> If degeneration is the dark, regressive side of progress, then regeneration is the reformation—the spiritual and physical renewal—but only of those by nature fit for it. And gentrification is the form of regeneration which most readily defines the post-modern city. Gentrification is a structural phenomenon tied to changing forms of capital accumulation and the means of maximizing ground rent. It involves tax-assisted displacement of longtime inner-city resident poor (usually the racially marginalized), renovation of the vacated residential space, upscaling the neighborhood, and resettling the area with inhabitants of higher socioeconomic status. (1993:201)

Underlying notions like redevelopment and gentrification is the discourse of development. Although much of the critical work on the discourse of development has focused on the "Third World," it is useful in terms of developing a pedagogy of place, particularly in the context of the urban, in that it would reaffirm the need of a pedagogy of place to reveal how the redevelopment of space in the city is dependent upon constructing a racial Other. According to Arturo Escobar, development is not only an instrument of economic control over the physical and social reality of much of Asia, Africa, and Latin America, it is also an "invention and strategy produced by the 'First World' about the 'underdevelopment of the 'Third World'" (1992:22). Escobar goes on to point out, "Development has been the primary mechanism through which these parts of the world have been produced and have produced themselves, thus marginalizing or precluding other ways of seeing and doing" (1992:22). This is of particular significance given that the discourse of development is connoted with growth, evolution, and maturation. Or as Escobar states, "The problem is complicated by the fact that the post-World War II discourse of development is firmly entrenched in Western modernity and economy" (1992:22).

What Escobar's critique of the discourse of development suggests for a pedagogy of place is that it must work with inner-city blacks in terms of how they see redevelopment. A pedagogy of place must link struggles over the definition of blackness and black identity with struggles over the image of redevelopment, with how those images construct racialized spaces and racialized Others. Though he does not talk about a pedagogy of place, Mel King recognizes the importance of why black urban struggles must deal with how black people think about themselves and what that means for the control of land by black urban communities. He writes,

> I would like to challenge people to think differently about strategies of shaping the future of cities. We are faced with a struggle for land and a struggle for the mind. This is the core of urban community organizing today, and I think it is crucial. It is my contention that, if we win the struggle for the mind, then we will win the struggle for the land. So, we

have to think about where the struggle for the mind exists. Obviously, we have to deal with the issue of race. (1991:1)

King's comments indicate that it is important for a pedagogy of place to link black self-definition to how blacks define and use public space in the city. This means that the starting point for a pedagogy of place is with the "voices" of inner-city blacks. According to Henry Giroux, "The concept of voice represents forms of self and social representation that mediate and produce wider structures of meaning, experience, and history" (1991:100). Through the concept of voice, a pedagogy of place can help blacks become more self-reflective about the construction of their racial identities, particularly when pertaining to their living spaces in the city. The concern then is with how white supremacist definitions of black public spaces shape not only black identities but also how blacks relate to the redevelopment of their spaces in the city. As Michele Wallace notes, black struggles over self-image are overwhelmingly directed towards trying to "salvage the denigrated image of blacks in the white imagination" (1990:2). Related to this, the binary logic of white supremacy sets limits on black struggles for identity and dignity, in that these struggles are defined in relation to "positive" versus "negative" images. One problem with this is that "positive images" are the bipolar opposites of negative, degrading stereotypes put forward by white supremacist ideologies. Struggles by blacks to represent themselves in a "positive" image make them complicitous in the maintenance of white supremacy, since white norms and standards define positive images. In agreement Wallace writes that

> since racism or the widespread conviction that blacks are morally and/or intellectually inferior, defines the "commonsense" perception of blacks, a positive /negative image cultural formula means that the goal of cultural production becomes simply to reverse these already existing assumptions. Not only

does reversal, or the notion that blacks are more like-able, more compassionate, smarter, or even "supe-rior," not substantially alter racist preconceptions, it also ties Afro-American cultural production to racist ideology in a way that makes the failure to alter it inevitable. (1991:2)

Wallace's critique of positive/negative images must also be extended to the cultural production of place. What her critique suggests for a pedagogy of place is that it must pay close attention to how the manufacturing of place by blacks is configured around blacks' desire for not only a "positive" image of themselves, but of their neighborhoods. A peda-gogy of place must therefore help blacks understand how their struggle for a "positive image of place" is compro-mised by white racist stereotypes that construct and fuel black self-contempt. In addition to this, a pedagogy of place must address how black self-contempt, when expressed in terms of wanting a "positive image of place," can even be complicitous with police repression and redevelopment strategies that deterritorialize and evict some blacks from the city. Again, Logan and Molotch argue, "From the stand-point of the community organization, and this is indeed a paradox, it becomes necessary to destroy at least part of the neighborhood in order to save it" (1987:145). They are sug-gesting that the displacement of "undesirables" from black neighborhoods is believed by many black community orga-nizers to be necessary to begin constructing a "positive image of place," which in turn will raise property values and bring more businesses, jobs, and the middle-class to the area. The belief of organizers, say Logan and Molotch, is that "the community can only be saved by treating it as a commodity" (1987:145).

Finally, assimilationist and Afrocentric notions of black identity have generally informed "positive images of place" in black urban communities. In addition, both notions are informed by the binary logic of white supremacy. Assimilationist notions of place are informed by the ideology of Liberal individualism, more specifically by the civil rights movement's "color-blind" consciousness. The color-blind consciousness stance of the civil rights movement represented a Eurocentric-oriented assimilationist racial consciousness. This position Cornel West argues "set out to show that black people were really like white people—thereby eliding differences (in history, culture) between blacks and whites. Black specificity and particularity were thus banished in order to gain white acceptance and approval" (1993:17). The argument of the assimilationist is that when blacks, particularly poor working-class inner-city blacks, are geographically concentrated in the same territory due to residential and employment racial segregation, they perpetuate crime, violence, single-parent households, and a cycle of poverty. From this perspective then one can understand why mainstream black scholars and leaders have shown concern over the exodus of the black middle class. They argue that this exodus has not only meant a loss in economic terms, but also in social terms. Their assumption is that the black middle class historically has been responsible for extending mainstream values to poor working-class urban blacks like family patterns and work ethics (Wilson, 1987). Assimilationist notions of place have generally supported redevelopment efforts with the hopes that this would spatially deconcentrate and integrate the "desirable" urban poor into middle-class neighborhoods, whether black or white.

Afrocentric or essentialist notions of black identity are informed racial unity. As important is the concept of self-determination, that blacks must lead and run their own organizations—that blacks can do things themselves. Related to this is the idea that "black people [should] consolidate behind their own, so that they can bargain from a position of strength" (Dyson, 1993:47). Although the concept of black self-determination it is not specific to Afrocentrism, its particular formulation by Afrocentrism is informed by a "homogeneous" notion of racial unity. It argues that a precondition for black unity is that blacks become aware that they have a history that predates slavery, one that begins on the continent of Africa. Another way of putting this is that black unity is dependent upon blacks tracing their "roots" to Africa. Michael Dyson points out that this search for racial unity has to do with "the desperate effort to replace a cultural uprooting that should have never occurred with a racial unanimity that never existed" (1993:xv). Dyson later goes on to state that while clan, community, and nation were central to African societies, only a cultural catastrophe the magnitude of chattel slavery could impose upon blacks an artificial and single racial identity (1993:xv). Motivating the quest for racial unity is the desire to preserve community life before the colonizers intervened, thus the assumption is that the future is in the past (Pieterse, 1992:12).

The Afrocentric world view therefore is to search for fixed, transcendental notions of black culture and blackness. It also believes that if black people are aware of their African roots, they would have much better self-esteem, subsequently giving them confidence to compete with their white counterparts for the American Dream—to be entrepreneurs. In addition to this, Afrocentrism has opportunistically supported the corporate redevelopment of city space as a strategy to promote black capitalism within the public spaces of the black community. This strategy has been accompanied by desire to commodify black culture, making black cultural products the basis for black capitalism, in the form of exotic black American or African restaurants, upscale jazz and blues clubs, African boutiques and art galleries, and music stores. The primary concern is to make the physical space of the black community attractive for private investment, consequently marginalizing or displacing poor working-class urban blacks (Allen, 1970). What was once an inner-city black community becomes an upscale middle-class white and black neighborhood. The implication is that the private use of black public spaces represents an attempt by black entrepreneurs, armed with the ideology of black unity, to control the political dialogue about how the "ghetto" territory should be used and defined. In a sense, the essentialist discourse of Afrocentrism is linked to an exclusionary definition and use of black urban space, to a positive image of place that is occupied by black capitalism.

For a pedagogy of place to move beyond the assimilationist versus Afrocentric dualism, it must be linked with a politics of decolonization, to the creation of new meanings of blackness and black identity. Decolonization implies a "process of cultural and historical liberation; an act of confrontation with a dominant system of thought" (hooks, 1992:1). This contestating white supremacist systems of thought and values goes beyond addressing black self-hatred to linking political resistance, in this case, black urban resistance, to loving blackness (hooks, 1992b). According to bell hooks, "loving blackness" is a "political stance" because as a sign, blackness "primarily evokes in the public imagination of whites hatred and fear" (1992b:100). She states that "to love blackness is dangerous in a white supremacist culture—so threatening, so serious a breach in the fabric of the social order, that death is the punishment" (1992b).

A pedagogy of place must also link the process of decolonization—the loving of blackness—to the complex and contradictory positioning of the black subject. More specifically, it has to challenge the colonizing logic of white supremacist culture by first acknowledging the multiple identifications and experiences of the black subject; it must understand that locations in gender, class, race, ethnicity and sexuality complicate one another and not merely additively" (Smith and Watson, 1992:xiv). Thus, the colonizing logic of white supremacy "implies a relation of structural domination and a suppression—often violent—of the heterogeneity of the [black] subject" (Mohanty and Mohanty, 1990:19). Restated, the colonizing project of white supremacist culture is related to the containment of difference by creating an essentialist and unified notion of racial identity (Smith and Watson, 1993). Decolonization implies various colonialisms or systems of racial dominations. As Cornel West notes, "racist treatment vastly differs owing to class, gender, sexual orientation, nation, region, hue and age" (1991a:28). This particular underlying assumption of decolonization has led some black feminists to challenge homogenized notions of blackness. They argue that homogenized notions of blackness are about black men gaining access to patriarchy through material privilege:

> And even though the more radical 1960s black power movement repudiated imitation of whites, emphasizing Pan-Africanist connections, their vision of liberation was not particularly distinctive or revolutionary . . . liberatory efforts centered around gaining access to material privilege, the kind of nation-building which would place black men in position of authority and power. (hooks, 1990:16)

In contrast to homogeneous constructions of black identity, bell hooks recognizes "the primacy of identity politics as an important stage in the liberation process," and proposes the notion of "radical black subjectivity" (1990:18). She uses this term to denote radical efforts to subvert static notions of black identity as a way to make visible "the complexity and variety to constructions of black subjectivity." Her equating radical black subjectivity with heterogeneity and not static notions of black identity moves black resistance from one of opposition to one of self-actualization:

> How do we create an oppositional world-view, a consciousness, an identity, a standpoint that exists not only as the struggle which also opposes dehumanization but as that movement which enables creative, expansive self-actualization. Opposition is not enough. In that vacant space after one has resisted there is still the necessity to become—to make oneself anew. That process emerges as one comes to understand how structures of domination work in one's own life, as one develops critical thinking and critical consciousness, as one invents new, alterna-

tive habits of being, and resist from that marginal space of difference inwardly defined. (1990:15)

Hooks' reconceptualizing black identity around a "radical black subjectivity" is therefore opposed to static and one-dimensional notions of identity that construct black resistance in relation to binary oppositions. In this instance, black resistance involves replacing "negative" interpretations of stereotypical characterizations of blacks with "positive" ones. Nevertheless, the stereotype remains intact. In conjunction with this process is also an inversion whereby "black culture" is seen as superior to "white culture," as in the case of Afrocentricism. Within this mode of black resistance, both cultures are viewed as separate, distinct, and incompatible suggesting a notion of racial authenticity.

This search for authentic or essentialist constructions of blackness and black culture is in contradiction to a notion of resistance linked to emancipation. What is important about this linkage is that resistance is not simply reduced to a politics of oppositionality but to one of self-actualizations. This is because emancipation is "not simply about saying no, reacting, refusing, but also and primarily about social creativity, introducing new values and aims, new forms of co-operation and action" (Pieterse, 1992:13). In this way, black resistance becomes tied to a politics of identity that is transformative, a politics that moves beyond defining blackness within the white supremacist framework of binary oppositions. Although the concept of emancipation is an important corrective in redefining black resistance, there is also an aspect of it that is problematic, that is, its roots in the totalizing narratives of Western modernity. This is because in the Eurocentric, Western humanist tradition what dominates is the idea of the universality of fundamental human experiences, that experiences are identical, regardless of their wide cultural and historical differences, that underneath there is one human nature and therefore one common human essence. The assimilationist discourse is compatible with this idea of emancipation.

What is important about the concepts of decolonization, emancipation, and hooks' notion of "radical black subjectivity" is that they provide us with a way to talk about black public spaces in the city not simply as "spaces of opposition" but as "spaces of self-actualization." In this way, defining black public spaces as "places of self-actualization" is understanding the centrality of black popular urban culture in constructing such places. For one thing, it is through black popular culture that black people in the city resist mainstream white culture's racializing and therefore biologization of their spaces, bodies, and personalities. This is important in that the early twentieth-century construction of the city as jungle—an image that preceded the emergence of large-scale black urban settlements—is now connoted with black people's dark skin. In other words, the urban has become a metaphor for race, and in a white supremacist culture, like ours, race does not mean white, but black. So, in the city, urban problems, such as poverty, homelessness, joblessness, crime, violence, single-parent households, and drugs, are seen as racial problems, the problems of blacks, not of whites. And in a white supremacist culture, where race is biologized, racial problems are reduced to black people's bodies. In a sense, then, black urban popular culture attempts to construct new meanings of blackness, one that historicizes race and subsequently blackness and the spaces that blacks occupy in the city (Gilroy, 1991).

Black urban popular culture is the "voice" of the black urban movement (Gilroy, 1991:223). What distinguishes black urban social movements from working-class movements, the labor movement, for example, is that political action and organization take place outside of the workplace's political economy (Tourine, 1988; Melucci, 1989; Gilroy, 1991). Transforming the United States from an industrial to a post-industrial capitalist society has turned blacks into a surplus population, into an expendable population, making them useless in terms of the economy. In the context of postindustrial capitalism, automation, cybernetics, neo-liberal austerity, state policies, and white racism within the labor movement have contributed to mass urban black unemployment and underemployment. Subsequently, then, the factory is not the site from which blacks develop black consciousness and solidarity. It is in their settlement spaces in the the city, their homeplaces, where the process of self-actualization occurs.

New social movement theorists, such as Alberto Melucci, Alain Tourine, and Paul Gilroy, point out that one of the key features of new movements is their alternative public spaces. Melucci refers to the public spaces of new social movements as "invisible networks of small groups submerged in everyday life. These submerged networks constitute the "laboratories" where new experiences are invented and movements question and challenge the dominant codes of everyday life (Melucci, 1989:6). In the preface to Melucci's book, *Nomads of the Present*, John Keane and Paul Mier write, "These laboratories are places in which the elements of everyday life are mixed, developed and tested, a site in which reality is given new names and citizens can develop alternative experiences of time, space and interpersonal relations" (Melucci, 1989:6). Using his concept of historicity, Tourine argues that new social movements "act upon themselves"; that is, through their cultural models they represent themselves and their actions, and in so doing challenge dominant cultural codes. Melucci similarly argues that new social movements are, in his words, "self-referential," they "are not just instrumental for their goals, they are a goal in themselves" (1989:60). For new social movements, then, the reference for social struggle is not the political system or state. This is not to say that social and political forms of struggle are not combined, but that new social movements link demands for inclusion and rights for the excluded group with the affirmation of difference. Gilroy elaborates this point by saying that

> new social movements are not primarily oriented
> towards instrumental objectives, such as the con-

quest of political power or state apparatuses, but rather towards control of a field of autonomy or independence vis a vis the system and the immediate satisfaction of collective desires. . . . The very refusal to accept mediation be the existing frameworks and institutions of the political system or to allow strategy to be dominated by the task of winning power within it, provides these movements with an important focus of group identity. (1987:226)

Melucci's, Tourine's, and Gilroy's comments about new social movements help us to recognize that it is inside the spaces of black urban settlements that blacks create new cultural models, new ways of experiencing and identifying with blackness. Black public spaces in the city challenge the cultural codes of white supremacy, and to quote bell hooks, "Loving blackness is a political stance"; "loving blackness is dangerous in a white supremacist culture" (1992:100). Because the black body has been the primary site for white supremacist repression and cultural denigration—constructing blacks as the dangerous Other, particularly in cities—it has also been the site from which black people have resisted. In support, Paul Gilroy argues that like the women's movement the gay and lesbian movement, and sections of the peace movement, issues around the body as well play a fundamental, definitive role in black urban social movements:

Blacks who live in the castle of their skin and have struggled to escape the biologization of their socially and politically constructed subordination are already sensitive to this issue. The attempt to articulate blackness as an historical rather than as a natural category confronts reality. The escape from bestial status into a recognized humanity has been a source of both ethics and politics since the slave system was first instituted. Black artists have thus identified the body as a seat of desires and as a nexus of interpersonal relationships in a special way which expresses the aspiration that skin colour will one day be no more significant than eye pigment and, in the meantime, announces that black is beautiful. (1991:226-227)

Gilroy's mention of black cultural workers seems to imply that through black popular culture, blacks resist and construct new meanings of blackness in relation to their bodies. It is black popular culture's deliberate use of the body as a canvas, particularly through its production of style and music, that has allowed blacks to attach new meanings of blackness to their bodies (Hall, 1992:27). According to Jefferies, style, music, and the body as a canvas, are three repertoires of black popular culture, and the city is a fourth. This is the place where black popular culture is born (Jefferies, 1992:27). The city is the place where the "language of black popular culture describes the emotions and circumstances black urban resistance encounters" (Jefferies, 1992:27). These circumstances include the control of black bodies through the manipulation of urban space (the redevelopment of space or gentrification), the surveillance and repression of black bodies through state sanctioned and organized policing, and the coercive control of black bodies in the work process (Gilroy, 1991).

Finally, a pedagogy of place for black urban struggle must use black urban popular culture as a way to recall black people's circumstances. This means that through black urban popular culture a pedagogy of place connects the voices of urban blacks to their narratives about the city. According to McLaren, "Narratives help us remember and also forget. They help shape our social reality as much by what they exclude as what they include" (1993a:140). And, because the self is constituted in relation to multiple narratives, its contradictions and consistencies provide the context for understanding how the narratives we construct to explain our experiences marginalize and silence differences. In support of this view, Henry Giroux writes that a "viable critical pedagogy needs to [anaylze] how ideologies are actually taken up in the voices and lived experiences of students as they give meaning to dreams, desires, and subject positions they inhabit" (1992a:169). He concludes by saying that "radical educators need to provide conditions for students to speak so that their narratives can be affirmed and engaged along with the consistencies and contradictions that characterize such experiences" (1992:169). Only by doing this can a pedagogy of place help urban blacks create what McLaren (1993a:140) calls a "critical narratology." By this McLaren "means reading personal narratives against society's treasured stock of narratives, since not all narratives share a similar status and there are those which exist devalued within society's rifts and margins" (1993a:140). The significance of this is that "critical narratology" can provide insights into how particular notions of difference—for instance, the binarism used by white supremacist culture to racialize the urban spaces of blacks—promote essentialist notions of blackness. Therefore, McLaren proposes that "the construction of narrative identities of liberation places a central emphasis on the meaning of difference" (1993:217). McLaren addresses this same issue when he calls for critical pedagogy to be linked to "critical multiculturalism," because critical multiculturalism highlights how the construction of difference around binarisms permits "whiteness to serve as an invisible norm against which to measure the worth of other cultures" (McLaren, 1992b:339). A pedagogy based upon critical multiculturalism is therefore relevant regarding how the invisible norm of whiteness is the narrative that informs "images of redevelopment."

Henry Giroux's notion of a critical "pedagogy of representation" and a "representational pedagogy" brings to surface similar issues regarding "the relationship between identity and culture, particularly as it is addressed in the discourse of racial difference" (1994:33). As Giroux has noted, "the identity politics of the right-wing in its attempt to block progressive political possibilities privileg[es] race as a sign of social disorder and civic decay" (1994:37). He argues that within the racial discourse of the right, "whiteness is not only privileged, it is also the only referent for social change, hope and action" (1994: 45). Giroux argues, like McLaren, that whiteness is able to represent itself in this way by positioning itself as the invisible norm. A pedagogy of representation for Giroux must therefore focus on demystifying representations of racial difference by revealing whose identity, history, social forms and ethics, and view of knowledge and consensus within unequal relations of power is narrating the storyline. The primacy of a pedagogy of representation is that images of redevelopment become linked to questions of subjectivity, power, and politics, but even more important, they would be increasingly significant as pedagogical practices (Giroux, 1994:47). A pedagogy of representation is useful for developing a pedagogy for black urban struggle in that it suggests that blacks must analyze those myth-making institutions in the city that rewrite the histories of race and colonialism in the material landscape of the city (Giroux, 1994:47). Representational pedagogy, on the other hand, focuses less on the "structuring principles that inform the form and content of the representation of politics [and more on] how students and others learn to identify, challenge, and rewrite such representations" (Giroux, 1994:50). This means that a pedagogy of black urban struggles would focus on recoverying new notions of blackness by looking at how black identities have been historically constructed in the city, particularly in relation to the spatial structure of the city. Blacks and others would look at how blacks have historically constructed transformative notions of blackness that recall memories of how blacks have used their living spaces to create communities of resistance. Representational pedagogy of black urban struggle would highlight the fact that black identity and black living spaces are not fixed and static. Such a pedagogy would counter the racialization of residential space through the imagery of racial segregation, an imagery that suggests that the problems experienced by black people are sharply bounded in space or that when blacks live in the same geographical area they produce social pathologies (Smith, Susan, 1993).

Furthermore, a pedagogy of black urban struggle must understand that narratives are not only constituted in relation to meaning but also around the body. Another way of putting this is that experience is not only about what is interpreted, but also about the pain and anguish felt in and on the bodies of the oppressed when deterritorialized by redevelopment and policed. The narratives that are expressed by black urban popular culture are also about the black body. Cornel West notes, "Black cultural practices emerge out of an acknowledgement of a reality they cannot not know—the ragged edges of the real, of necessity, . . . of not being able to eat, not having shelter, not having health care" (1989:89). It is "the ragged edges of the real" that shape the popular vernacular of blacks, therefore organizing the narratives and meanings they give to their lived experiences. In this way, the body plays an important role in the formation of black identity. McLaren reminds us that "[w]e cannot separate the body from the social formation, since the material density of all forms of subjectivity is achieved through the micropractices of power that are socially inscribed into our flesh" (1992:5).

It is in this context that a pedagogy for black urban struggle takes up questions regarding the black body/subject. McLaren's use of the term *body/subject* refers to "a terrain of the flesh in which meaning is inscribed, constructed, and reconstituted" (1991:150). That is, "the body [must be] conceived as the interface of the individual and society, as a site of embodied or enfleshed subjectivity which also reflects the ideological sedimentations of the social structure inscribed into it" (McLaren, 1991:150). How then do these "ideological sedimentations of the social structure regulate the black body subject? What is implied in this question is that the theoretical knowledges contained in ideologies "constitute externalized metaphors of the body" (McLaren, 1991:13). In a white supremacist culture, not only do "externalized metaphors" racialize the bodies and public spaces of blacks and establish a pretext for deterritorialization, but they also become the basis for black self-contempt.

This suggests that a pedagogy of black urban struggle be tied to Giroux's representational pedagogy: "Central to such an approach is understanding how knowledge and desire come together to promote particular forms of cultural production, investments, and counter-narratives that invoke communities of memory that are lived, felt and interrogated" (1994:51). A pedagogy of black urban struggle linked to a representational pedagogy would recognize that black self-contempt is the result of blacks essentializing (e.g., biologizing their bodies, using white supremacist definitions of race and blackness). For example, such a pedagogy would point out how phallocentric models of black masculinity, certain constructions of black femininity and of the black poor by middle-class blacks are informed by white supremacist notions about the black body (hooks, 1992; Ransby and Matthews, 1993). In addition to this, a pedagogy of place for black urban struggle would take seriously questions around the body and how mainstream white consumer culture's exoticizing of the black body has reinforced both black self-hatred and the market values of individualism, consumerism, and competiveness. It is the values and assumptions that inform white supremacy and mainstream white consumer culture that a pedagogy of place for black urban struggle must critically interrogate in terms of their influences on the formation of black identity and black public spaces in the city.

Bibliography

Adero, Malaika. 1993. *Up South: Stories, Studies, and Letters of this Century's African American Migration.* New York: The New Press.

Allen, Robert. 1970. *Black Awakening in Capitalist America.* New York: Anchor Books.

Armstrong, Philip, Kelley Dennis, and Bradley J. Macdonald. 1990. "Introduction: Raising the City." In *Strategies: A Journal of Theory, Culture and Politics.* Number 3.

Aronowitz, Stanley. 1990. *The Crisis in Historical Materialism: Class, Politics and Culture in Marxist Theory.* Minneapolis: University of Minnesota Press.

Aronowitz, Stanley, and Giroux, Henry A. 1991. *Postmodern Education: Politics, Culture, and Social Criticism.* Minneapolis: University of Minnesota Press.

Bailey, Cameron. 1988. "Nigger/Lover: The Thin Sheen of Race in 'Something Wild.'" In *Screen.* Volume 29, Number 4.

Baker, Jr., Houston A. 1984. *Blues, Ideology, and Afro-American Literature: A Venacular Theory.* Chicago: The University of Chicago Press.

Banfield, Edward C. 1968. *The Unheavenly City Revisited.* Boston: Little, Brown and Company.

Baudrillard, J. 1981. *For a Political Economy of the Sign.* St. Louis: Telos Press.

Beauregard, Roger A. 1986. "The Chaos and Complexity of Gentrification." In Neil Smith and Peter Williams (eds.), *Gentrification and the City.* Boston: Allen & Unwin.

Bellah, Robert. 1985. *Habits of the Heart*. Berkeley: University of California.

Boggs, James. 1970. *Racism and the Class Struggle: Further Pages from a Black Worker's Notebook*. New York: Monthly Review.

Boyer, M. Christine. 1986. *Dreaming the Rational City*. Cambridge, MA: The MIT Press.

———. 1990. "The Return of Aestheitcs to City Planning." In Dennis Crows, *Phiosophical Streets: New Approaches to Urbanism*. Washington, D.C.:Maisonneuve Press.

Bush, Rod. 1984. *The New Black Vote*. San Francisco: Synthesis Publications.

Carby, Hazel. 1989. "The Canon: Civil War and Reconstruction." In *Michigan Quarterly Review*. Volume 28.

Carmichael, Stokely, and Charles V. Hamilton. 1967. *Black Power: The Politics of Liberation*. New York: Vintage Press.

Castells, Manuel. 1983. *The City and the Grassroots*. Berkeley: University of California Press.

Clay, Philip. 1978. *Neighborhood Revitalization: Issues, Trends, and Strategies*. Cambridge: Massachusetts Institute of Technology.

Clifford, James. 1988. *The Predictment of Culture: Twentieth-Century Ethnography, Literature, and Art*. Cambridge: Harvard University Press.

Cross, Michael, and Michael Keith. 1993. "Racism and the Postmodern City." In Michael Keith and Malcolm Cross, *Racism, the City and the State*. New York: Routledge.

Crow, Dennis. 1990. *Philosophical Streets: New Approaches to Urbanism*. Washington, D.C.: Maisonneuve Press.

Davis, Mike. 1986. *Prisoners of the American Dream*. London: Verso.

———. 1990. *City of Quartz: Excavating the Future in Los Angeles*. London: Verso.

———. 1992. "Fortress Los Angeles: The Militarization of Urban Space." In Michael Sorkin (ed.), *Variations on a Theme Park: The New American City and the End of Public Space*. New York: The Noonday Press.

Dent, Gina. 1992. "Black Pleasure, Black Joy: An Introduction." In Gina Dent (ed.), *Black Popular Culure*. Seattle: Bay Press.

Deutsche, Rosalyn. 1991a. "Alternative Space." In Brian Wallis (ed.) *If You Lived Here: The City in Art, Theory, and Social Activism*. Seattle: Seattle Bay Press.

———. 1991b. "Architecture of the Evicted." In Strategies: *A Journal of Theory, Culture and Politics*. No. 3.

———. 1991c. "Men in Space." In *Strategies: A Journal of Theory, Culture and Politics*. No. 3.

———. 1991d. "Uneven Development: Public Art in New York." In Diane Ghirardo (ed.), *A Social Out of Site Criticism of Architecture*. Seattle: Seattle Bay Press.

Drake, St. Clair, and Horace R. Cayton. 1962. *Black Metropolis: A Study of Negro Life in a Northern City*. New York: Harper and Row.

Dyer, Richard. 1988. "White." In *Screen*. Volume 29, Number 4.

Dyson, Michael Eric. 1993. *Reflecting Black: African American Cultural Criticism*. Minneapolis: University of Minnesota Press.

Ehrenreich, Barbara. 1989. *Fear of Falling: The Inner Life of the Middle Class*. New York: HarperCollins Publishers.

Entrikin, J. Nicholas. 1991. *The Betweenness of Place: Towards a Geography of Modernity*. Baltimore: The Johns Hopkins University Press.

Epps, Archie. 1991. *Malcolm X: Speeches at Harvard*. New York: Paragon House.

Escobar, Arturo. 1992. "Imagining a Post-Development Era? Critical Thought, Development and Social Movement." In *Social Text*. No. 31/32.

Evans-Butler, Elliott. 1989. *Race, Gender and Desire: Narrative Strategies in the Fiction of Toni Cade Bambara, Toni Morrison, Alice Walker.* Philadelphia: Temple University Press.

Ewen, Stuart. 1976. *Captains of Consciousness: Advertising and the Social Roots of the Consumer Culture.* New York: McGraw-Hill Book Company.

Folch-Seria, M. 1990. "Place, Voice, Space: Mikhail Bakhtin's Dialogical Landscape." In *Environment and Planning D: Society and Space.* Volume 8, Number 3.

Fordham, Signithia. 1988. "Racelessness as a Factor in Black Students' School Success: Pragmatic Strategy or Pyrrhic Victory?" In *Harvard Educational Review* 59(1), 54-84.

Frampton, Kenneth. 1988. "Place-Form and Cultural Identity." In John Thackara, *Design After Modernism.* New York: Thames and Hudson.

Fraser, Nancy. 1991. "Rethinking the Public Sphere: A Contribution to the Critique of Actually Existing Democracy." In *Social Text.* Spring.

Freire, Paulo. 1992. *Pedagogy of the Oppressed.* New York: Continuum.

Friedland, Roger. 1992. "Space, Place and Modernity." In *A Journal of Reviews: Contemporary Sociology.* Volume 21, Number 1.

Gilman, Sander L. 1985. *Difference and Pathology: Stereotypes of Sexuality, Race, and Madness.* Ithaca, NY: Cornell University Press.

Gilroy, Paul. 1991. *"There Ain't No Black in the Union Jack": The Cultural Politics of Race and Nation.* Chicago: The University of Chicago Press.

Giroux, Henry A. 1983. *Theory and Resistance in Education: A Pedagogy for the Opposition.* South Hadley: Bergin and Garvey.

———. 1991. *Postmodernism, Feminism, and Cultural Politics: Redrawing the Educational Boundaries.* Albany: State University of New York Press.

———. 1992a. *Border Crossings: Cultural Workers and the Politics of Education.* New York: Routledge, Chapman, and Hall, Inc.

———. 1992b. "Language, Difference, and Curriculum Theory: Beyond the Politics of Clarity." In *Theory into Practice.*

———. 1993. *Living Dangerously: Multiculturalism and the Politics of Difference.* New York: Peter Lang Press.

———. 1994. "Living Dangerously: Identity Politics and the New Cultural Racism." In Henry A. Giroux and Peter McLaren (eds.) *Between Borders: Pedagogy and the Politics of Cultural Studies.* New York: Routledge.

Goldberg, David Theo (ed.). 1990. *Anatomy of Racism.* Minneapolis: University of Minnesota Press.

———. 1993. *Racist Culture: Philosophy and the Politics of Meaning.* Cambridge, MA: Basil Blackwell Inc.

Goldman, Robert, and Steve Papson. 1991. "Levis and the Knowing Wink." In *Current Perspectives in Social Theory.* Volume II.

Gordon, David M. 1978. "Capitalist Develoment and the History of American Cities." In William Tabb and Larry Sawers (eds.), *Marxism and the Metropolis.* New York: Oxford University Press.

Gorz, André. 1982. *Farewell to the Working Class: An Essay on Post-industrial Sociolism.* Boston: Southend Press.

———. 1989. *Critique of Economic Reason.* New York: Verso.

Gottdiener, M. 1985. *The Social Production of Urban Space.* Austin: University of Austin.

Grossberg, Lawrence, Cary Nelson, Paula A. Treichler (eds.). 1992. *Cultural Studies.* New York: Routledge.

Hall, Stuart. 1991. "Ethnicity: Identity and Difference." In *Radical America.* Volume 23, Number 4.

———. 1992. "What Is This 'Black' in Black Popular Culture." In Gina Dent, *Black Popular Culture.* Seattle: Bay Press.

Hall, Stuart, and Martin Jacques. 1990. "The New Times: Manifesto for New Times." In New Times: *The Changing Face of Poltics in the 1990s*. London: Verso.

Hall, Stuart, and Tony Jefferson (eds.). 1976. *Resistance through Rituals: Youth Subcultures in Post-War Britain*. London: Hutchinson.

Hamilton, Cynthia. 1988. "Apartheid in an American City." In *LA Weekly*. December 30.

———. 1991. "The Loss of Community and Women's Space." In *Canadian Woman Studies/Les Cahiers De La Femme*.

Harvey, David. 1973. *Social Justice and the City*. Baltimore: John Hopkins University Press.

———. 1989. *The Urban Experience*. Baltimore: The Johns Hopkins University Press.

———. 1990a. "Between Space and Time: Reflections on the Geographical Imagination." In *Annals of the Association of American Geographers*. Volume 80(3), 418-34.

———. 1990b. *The Condition of Post Modernity: An Enquiry into the Origins of Cultural Change*. Cambridge, MA: Basil Blackwell, Inc.

———. 1991. "Flexibility: Threat or Opportunity." In Socialist Review. Volume 21, Number 1.

Hassan, Ihab. 1983. "Postmodernism: A Vanishing Horizon." Paper to Modern Language Association of America, New York.

Haymes, Stephen Nathan. 1991. "Pedagogy, Community Organizing, and American Populism." *Educational Foundations*. Volume 5, Number 3.

hooks, bell. 1990. *Yearning: Race, Gender, and Cultural Politics*. Boston: South End Press.

———. 1992a. "Representing Whiteness in the Black Imagination." In Lawrence Grossberg, Cary Nelson, and Paula Treichler (eds.), *Cultural Studies*. New York: Routledge.

———. 1992b. *Black Looks: Race and Representation*. Boston: Southend Press.

hooks, bell, and Cornel West. 1991. *Breaking Bread: Insurgent Black Intellectual Life*. Boston: South End Press.

Hummon, David M. 1990. *Commonplaces: Community Ideology and Identity in American Culture*. Albany: State University of New York Press.

Hutcheon, Linda. 1989. *The Politics of Postmodernism*. New York: Routledge.

Jager, Michael. 1986. "Class Definition and the Esthetics of Gentrification: Victoriana in Melbourne." In Neil Smith and Peter Williams, *Gentrification and the City*. Boston: Allen and Unwin.

Jefferies, John. 1992. "Toward a Redefinition of the Urban: The Collision of Culture." In Gina Dent, *Black Popular Culture*. Seattle: Bay Press.

Jenning, James. 1990. "The Politics of Black Empowerment in Urban America: Reflections on Race, Class and Community." In Joseph M. Kling and Prudence S. Posner, *Dilemmas of Activism: Class, Community, and the Politics of Local Mobilization*. Philadelphia: Temple University Press.

Jordon, Winthrop D. 1968. *White over Black*. New York: W. W. Norton & Company.

Julien, Issac, and Kobena Mercer. 1988. "Introduction: De Margin and de Centre." In *Screen*. Volume 29, Number 4.

Keil, Roger. 1990. "The Urban Revisited: Politics and Restructuring." In Strategies: *A Journal of Theory, Culture and Politics*. No. 3.

Keith, Michael. 1993. "From Punishment to Discipline? Racism, Racialization and the Policing of Social Control." In Michael Keith and Malcolm Cross, *Racism, the City and the State*. New York: Routledge.

Keith, Michael, and Steve Pile. 1993. *Place and the Politics of Identity*. New York: Routledge.

King, Mel. 1991. "A Framework for Action." In Philip W. Nyden and Wim Wiewel (eds.), *Challenging Uneven Development: An Urban Agenda for the 1990s*. New Brunswick: Rutgers University Press.

Kluge, Alexander. 1991. "The Public Sphere." In Brian Wallis (ed.), *If You Lived Here: The City in Art, Theory, and Social Activism*. Seattle: Bay Press.

Koptiuch, Kristin. 1991. "Third Worldizing at Home." In *Social Text*. Volume 9, Number 3.

Kovel, Joel. 1984. *White Racism: A Psychohistory*. New York: Columbia University Press.

Kozol, Jonathan. 1991. *Savage Inequality: Children in America's Schools*. New York: Crown Publishers, Inc.

Laclau, Ernesto. 1991. *New Reflections on the Revolution of Our Times*. London: Verso.

Langer, Peter. 1984. "Sociology—Four Images of Organized Diversity: Bazaar, Jungle, Organism, and Machine." In Rodwin and Hollister (eds.), *Cities of the Mind: Images and Themes of the City in Social Science*. New York: Plenum Press.

Lefebvre, Henri. 1974. *The Production of Space*. Cambridge, MA: Basil Blackwell, Inc.

————. 1977. "Reflections on the Politics of Space." In Richard Peet (ed.), *Radical Geography: Alternative Viewpoints on Contemporary Social Issues*. Chicago: Maaroufa Press, Inc.

————. 1979. "Space: Social Product and Use Value." In J. W. Freiberg (ed.), *Critical Sociology*. New York: Irvington Publishers, Inc.

————. 1990. *Everyday Life in the Modern World*. New Brunswick: Transaction Publishers.

Levitas, Ruth. 1990. *The Concept of Utopia*. Syracuse: Syracuse University Press.

Lipietz, Alain. 1987. *Mirages and Miracles: The Crisis of Global Fordism*. New York: Verso.

Logan, John R., and Harvey L. Molotch. 1987. *Urban Fortunes: The Political Economy of Place*. Los Angeles: University of California Press.

MacCannell, Dean. 1989. *The Tourist: A Theory of the Leisure Class*. New York: Schocken Books.

Macpherson, C. B. 1964. *The Political Theory of Possessive Individualism*. Oxford: Oxford University Press.

Marable, Manning. 1990. "A New Black Politics." In *Progressive Magazine*. August.

———. 1992a. "Black America in Search of Itself." In *Progressive Magazine*. November.

———. 1992b. *The Crisis of Color and Democracy*. Monroe, Maine: Common Courage Press.

Massey, Douglas S. and Nancy A. Denton. 1993. *American Apartheid: Segregation and the Making of the Underclass*. Cambridge, MA: Harvard University Press.

McLaren, Peter. 1989. *Life in Schools: An Introduction to Critical Pedagogy in the Foundations of Education*. New York: Longman.

———. 1991a. "Schooling the Postmodern Body: Critical Pedagogy and the Politics of Enfleshment." In Henry Giroux (ed.), *Postmodernism, Feminism, and Cultural Politics: Redrawing Educational Boundaries*. Albany: State University of New York Press.

———. 1991b. "Postmodernism, Postcolonialism and Pedagogy." In *Education and Society*. Volume 9, Number 2.

———. 1992a. "Collisions with Othernesss: 'Travelling' Theory, Post-Colonial Criticism, and the Politics of Ethnographic Practice—the Mission of the Wounded Ethnographer." In *Qualitative Studies in Education*. Volume 5, Number 1.

———. 1992b. "Critical Multiculturalism and Democratic Schooling: An Interview with Peter McLaren and Joe Kincheloe." In Shirley P. Steinberg, *International Journal of Educational Reform*.

———. 1993a. "Border Disputes: Multicultural Narrative, Identity Formation, and Critical Pedagogy in Postmodern America." In Daniel McLaughlin and William G. Tierney (eds.), *Naming Silence Lives: Personal Narratives and the Process of Educational Change*. New York: Routledge.

————. 1994. "Multiculturalism and the Postmodern Critique: Toward a Pedagogy of Resistance and Transformation." In Henry A. Giroux and Peter McLaren (eds.) *Between Borders: Pedagogy and the Politics of Cultural Studies.* New York: Routledge.

McLaren, Peter, and Peter Leonard (eds.). 1993. *Paulo Freire: A Critical Encounter.* New York: Routledge.

Melucci, Alberto. 1989. *Nomads of the Present: Social Movements and Individual Needs in Contemporary Society.* Philadelphia: Temple University Press.

Mercer, Kobena. 1990. "Introduction: De Margin and De Centre. In ICA Document 7, Black/British Cinema.

Mills C. A. 1988. "Life on the Upslope: Postmodern Landscape of Gentrification." In *Environment and Planning D: Society and Space.* Volume 6, 169-89.

Mohanty, Chandra T., and Satya Mohanty. 1990. "Contradictions of Colonialism," Women's Review of Books. March (7):19.

Mort, Frank. 1990. "The Politics of Consumption." In Stuart Hall and Martin Jacques (eds.), *New Times: The Changing Face of Politics in the 1990s.* London: Verso.

Mouffe, Chantal. 1988. "Hegemony and New Political Subjects: Toward a New Concept of Democracy." In Cary Nelson and Lawrence Grossberg, *Marxism and the Interpretation of Culture.* Urbana: University of Illinois Press.

Murray, Charles. 1984. *Losing Ground: American Social Policy, 1950-1980.* New York: Basic Books.

Murray, Robin. 1990. "Fordism and Post-Fordism." In Stuart Hall and Martin Jacques (eds.), *New Times: The Changing Face of Politics in the 1990s.* London: Verso.

Neal, Larry. 1989. *Visions of a Liberated Future: Black Arts Movement Writings.* New York: Thunder's Mouth Press.

Omi, Michael, and Howard Winant. 1986. *Racial Formation in the United States: From the 1960s to the 1980s.* New York: Routledge.

Parker, Anthony A. 1990. "Whose America Is It?" *Sojourners*. August/September.

Pictcrse, Jan Nederveen. 1992. "Emancipations, Modern and Postmodern." In *Development and Change*. Volume 23, Number 3.

Ransby, Barbara, and Tracy Matthews. 1993. "Black Popular Culture and the Transcendence of Patriarchal Illusions." In *Race and Class*. Volume 35, Number 1.

Reed, David. 1981. *Education for Building a People's Movement*. Boston: Southend Press.

Rosaldo, Renato. 1989. *Culture and Truth: The Remaking of Social Analysis*. Boston: Beacon Press.

Rose, Harold M. 1982. "The Future of the Black Ghettos." In Gary Gappert and Richard V. Knights (eds.), *Cities in the 21st Century*. Beverly Hills: Sage.

Rutherford, Jonathan (ed.). 1990. *Identity, Community, Culture, Difference*. London: Lawrence & Wishart Ltd.

Sack, Robert David. 1986. *Human Territoriality*. Cambridge: Cambridge University Press.

Sarup, Madan. 1989. *An Introduction Guide to Post-structuralism and Postmodernism*. Athens: The University of Georgia Press.

Saunders, Peter. 1986. *Social Theory and the Urban Question*. New York: Holmes & Meier Publishers, Inc.

Sentencing Project. 1991. *Americans Behind Bars: A Comparision of International Rates of Incarceration*. Washington, D.C.

Smith, Neil. 1984. *Uneven Development: Nature, Capital and the Production of Space*. Oxford: Basil Blackwell.

———. 1986. "Gentrification, the Frontier, and the Restructuring of Urban Space." In Neil Smith and Peter Williams (eds.), *Gentrification and the City*. Boston: Allen and Unwin.

———. 1987. "Of Yuppies and Housing: Gentrification, Social Restructuring, and the Urban Dream." In *Environment and Planning D: Society and Space*. Volume 5, 151-72.

————. 1992. "New City, New Frontier: The Lower East Side as Wild, Wild West." In Michael Sorkin (ed.), *Variations on a Theme Park: The New American City and the End of Public Space*. New York: The Noonday Press.

Smith, Neil, and Peter Williams. 1986. "Alternatives to Orthodoxy: Invitation to a Debate." In Neil Smith and Peter Williams (eds.), *Gentrification and the City*. Boston: Allen and Unwin.

Smith, Sidonie, and Julia Watson (eds.). 1992. *Decolonizing the Subject: The Politics of Gender in Women's Autobiography*. Minneapolis: University of Minnesota Press.

Smith, Susan J. 1993. "Residental Segregation and the Politics of Racialization." In Malcolm Cross and Michael Keith (eds.), *Racism, the City and the State*. New York: Routledge.

Soja, Edward W. 1989. *Postmodern Geographies: The Reassertation of Space in Critical Social Theory*. New York: Verso Press.

————. 1990. "Heterotopologies: A Rememberance of Other Spaces in Citadel-LA." In Strategies: *A Journal of Theory, Culture and Politics*. No. 3.

Sorkin, Michael. 1992. *Variations on a Theme Park: The New American City and the End of Public Space*. New York: Hill and Wang.

Sorkin, Sharon. 1991. *Landscapes of Power: From Detroit to Disney World*. Berkeley: Los Angeles Press.

Suttles, Gerald S. 1968. *The Social Order of the Slum: Ethnicity and Territory in the Inner City*. Chicago: The University of Chicago Press.

————. 1972. *The Social Construction of Communities*. Chicago: The University of Chicago Press.

Tabb, William K., and Larry Sawers. 1978. *Marxism and the Metropolis: New Perspectives in Urban Political Economy*. New York: Oxford University Press.

Taun, Yi-Fu. 1977. *Space and Place: The Perspective of Experience*. Minneapolis: University of Minnesota Press.

Taylor, Clyde. 1991. "The Re-Birth of the Aesthetic in Cinema." In *Wide Angle.* Volume 13, Numbers 3, 4.

Tourine, Alain. 1988. *Return of the Actor: Social Theory in Postindustrial Society.* Minneapolis: University of Minnesota Press.

Urban Strategies Group. 1992. "Call to Reject the Federal Weed and Seed Program in Los Angeles." A Project of the Labor/Community Strategy Center.

Wallace, Michele. 1990. *Invisibility Blues: From Pop to Theory.* London: Verso.

West, Cornel. 1982. *Prophesy Deliverance! An Afro-American Revolutionary Christianity.* Philadelphia: The Westminster Press.

———. 1988. "Interview with Cornel West." In Andrew Ross (ed.), *Universal Abandon! The Politics of Postmodernism.* Minneapolis: University of Minnesota Press.

———. 1989. "Black Culture and Postmodernism." In Barbara Kruger and Phil Mariani (eds.), *Remaking History.* Seattle: Bay Press.

———. 1991a. "The New Cultural Politics of Difference." In Russell Ferguson, Martha Gever, Trinh T. Minh-ha, and Cornel West (eds.), *Out There: Marginalization and Contemporary Cultures.* Cambridge, MA: The MIT Press.

———. 1991b. "Nihilism in Black America." In *Dissent.* Spring.

———. 1991c. "Princeton's Public Intellectual." In *New York Times Magazine.* September 15.

———. 1992. "Philosophy and the Underclass." In *The Underclass Question.* Philadelphia: Temple University Press.

Williams, Brett. 1988. *Upscaling Downtown: Stalled Gentrification in Washington D.C.* Ithaca: Cornell University Press.

Williams, Raymond. 1977. *Marxism and Literature.* Oxford: Oxford University Press.

Wilson, Elizabeth. 1991. *The Sphinx in the City: Urban Life, The Control of Disorder, and Women.* Berkeley: University of California Press.

Wilson, William J. 1987. *The Truly Disadvantaged.* Chicago: University Press.

Young, Loga. 1992. "A Nasty Piece of Work: A Psychoanalytic Study of Sexual and Racial Difference in 'Mona Lisa.'" In Jonathan Rutherford (ed.), *Identity: Community, Culture and Difference.* London: Lawernce and Wishart.

Zukin, Sharon. 1991. *Landscapes of Power: From Detroit to Disney World.* Berkeley: University of California Press.

Author Index

Subject Index

African American, xi-xv, xii, xiii. *See also* blacks

Afrocentricism, black culture and, 134, 137; black capitalism and, 134; positive images of place and, 132, 133-35; racial authenticity, 137; self-determination defined, 133

Alternative Public Space, 13. *See also* Black Public Sphere

American Fordism, Antonio Gramsci and, 61; crisis in, 37; mass advertisement and, 35, 36; mass production and mass consumption and 35, 36, 37; neofordism, 37; postfordist strategy, 38, 51

Architectural Redevelopment. *See* Gentrification

Assimilationism ideology of liberal integrationism, 30-31; western humanist tradition and, 137; positive images of place and, 132-33

Banfield's interpretation of black slums and urban riots, 121-22

Binary Logic. *See* Binary Opposition

Binary Opposition: black resistance and, 137; black settlement space and, 17, 72, 104; definition of, 45; stereotype and, 45, 46, 48; white supremacist ideologies and, 43, 45, 59, 131, 142

Bipolar Opposites. *See* Binary Opposition

Black America, ix

Black Civil Society, 27, 70, 71

Black Culture: black body and, 61, 63, 64, 115, 144; black city life and, 115, 116, 125; black identity, black consciousness, black subjectivity, black self-definition, ix, x, xi, xii, 9, 10, 11, 14, 17, 21, 36, 60; black imagination and, 54-55; black middle class and, 56-59; black nationalism and, 60, 64; blues, 61; black vernacular expression and, 53, 54, 60; critique of productivist ideology, anticapitalist themes and, 62; jazz, 62; Levi blue jeans ads and, 115;